ART-BASED GROUP THERAPY

ABOUT THE AUTHOR

Bruce L. Moon, Ph.D., ATR-BC, HLM, is a professor of art therapy, chair of the art therapy department, and director of the graduate art therapy program at Mount Mary College in Milwaukee, Wisconsin. He received the 2009 Honorary Life Member Award from the Buckeye Art Therapy Association and the 2007 Honorary Life Member Award from the American Art Therapy Association. Formerly the director of the graduate art therapy program at Marywood University in Scranton, Pennsylvania, and the Harding Graduate Clinical Art Therapy Program in Worthington, Ohio, he has extensive clinical, administrative, and teaching experience. He holds a doctorate in creative arts with specialization in art therapy from Union Institute in Cincinnati, Ohio. Moon's current clinical practice is focused on the treatment of emotionally disturbed adolescents. He has lectured and led workshops at many colleges, universities, conferences, and symposia in the United States and Canada.

Moon is author of *Existential Art Therapy; Essentials of Art Therapy Training and Practice; Introduction to Art Therapy; Art and Soul; The Dynamics of Art as Therapy with Adolescents; Ethical Issues in Art Therapy;* and *The Role of Metaphor in Art Therapy.* He is editor of *Working with Images: The Art of Art Therapists* and coeditor of *Word Pictures: The Poetry and Art of Art Therapists.* Moon's many years of experience in clinical and educational settings, coupled with his interdisciplinary training in art education, art therapy, theology, and creative arts, inspire his provocative theoretical and practical approach to art-based group therapy.

Author's Note

The clinical vignettes in this book are, in spirit, true. In all instances, details have been changed to ensure the confidentiality of persons with whom I have worked. The case illustrations and artworks presented are amalgamations of many specific situations. My intention is to provide realistic accounts of an art therapist's work with client groups while also protecting the privacy of individuals.

ART-BASED GROUP THERAPY

Theory and Practice

By

BRUCE L. MOON, PH.D., ATR-BC, HLM

CHARLES C THOMAS • PUBLISHER, LTD.
Springfield • Illinois • U.S.A.

Published and Distributed Throughout the World by

CHARLES C THOMAS • PUBLISHER, LTD.
2600 South First Street
Springfield, Illinois 62704

©2010 by CHARLES C THOMAS • PUBLISHER, LTD.

ISBN 978-0-398-07961-1 (paper)
ISBN 978-0-398-08315-1 (ebook)

Library of Congress Catalog Card Number: 2010022628

Printed in the United States of America
CR-R-3

Library of Congress Cataloging-in-Publication Data

Moon, Bruce L.
   Art-based group therapy : theory and practice / by Bruce L. Moon.
      p. cm.
   Includes bibliographical references and index.
   ISBN 978-0-398-07961-1 (pbk.)
   1. Art therapy. 2. Group psychotherapy. I. Title.
   [DNLM: 1. Art Therapy. 2. Group Therapy. WM 450.5.A8 M818ab 2010]

   RC489.A7M655 2010
   616.89'1656--dc22

                                                            2010022628

FOREWORD

They swaggered down the steps into the basement, making their way to the studio and looking more like a football team than a gathering of students at a therapeutic day school. Their saggy jeans and baggy jerseys accentuated their size; several had to duck to fit through the doorway. They thudded in along with their jackets, baseball hats, and portable CD players and slid into the chairs around the table.

Only three months out of graduate school, I started my career as an art therapist at a school program for troubled kids. As a graduate of an excellent art therapy program, I thought I was well prepared to lead groups, but nothing could have fully prepared me for my first experience. As I watched them take their places and swat at one another with their caps, I was beset by thoughts and questions: Remember to hold the space. How am I going to keep this environment safe? I hope they like me. What are we going to be doing today, again? These guys are really big, and they look very unhappy. I don't think they want to be here. Maybe I should have some music playing. Maybe I should have gotten a bigger table.

"So what are we going to make today?" one of the boys asked.

Before I could answer, another folded his arms, slouched into his chair, and exclaimed, "I hate this &!#%&*# art @$%!%."

And so it began.

Leading art therapy groups is often a challenge, but as Bruce Moon so eloquently describes in the following pages, making art in the context of others is an incredibly and almost inexplicably powerful experience. He writes, "Things happen for people in art therapy groups that really are almost magical." The author's approach is to simultaneously explore how this *magic* occurs while still honoring the mystery and power of interpersonal art making.

No human being is immune to the influence of other human beings. While we may choose to live in isolation, we are all social creatures, fundamentally linked and defined by our interactions with others (Siegel, 1999). Neuroscientists may argue that it is chemical, anthropologists that it is evolutionarily beneficial, but in any rationale, the power of the group is undeniable. Like most things that are powerful, group experiences entail multiple paradoxes. Within group dynamics lie opportunities for harm as well as healing. Moon argues that therapeutic opportunities reside in the fear, tension, and vulnerability inherent in the process of making art alongside others. While some art therapists may feel ambivalent about leading groups, the emotions and reactions the group experience evokes for both the leader and the client are often anything but neutral.

In addition to being powerful, art therapy group experiences are typically dynamic and complex, inspiring a multitude of questions and issues for the group leader. Group leaders must wrestle with such questions as: Should I have a directive? How structured should the group be and how open-ended? Do all the group members have to work on the same task or should they work individually? *What* do I say, *when* do I say it, and *how* should I say it? Do I have to use language at all? How is this particular project therapeutic?

The art therapy profession is in a time of promise and great potential. As the field continues to evolve and the work of art therapy enters into diverse milieus, foundations and supports that emphasize our "indigenous" resources are essential. As art therapy continues to grow, it also continues to learn how to support, advocate, and take care of itself. Moon encourages the art therapist to not look outside for validation, but rather to look from within. By placing the art at the center of practice, *Art-Based Group Therapy* creates an explanatory model and rationale for group practice that is rooted in art therapy theory and identity.

While indebted to the classic texts of Corey, Corey, and Corey (2008) and Yalom (2005), the author has not disposed of the more verbal-based explanations of group therapy, but rather has built an organic framework that is fundamentally rooted in art making. Moon suggests, "The main course of the therapeutic meal takes place among clients, media, process, and product. The essence of art therapy group work is beyond the expressive capacity of spoken words." Thus this book does not present a model of how art can be used alongside verbal processing within group situations to promote therapeutic change. It argues that *art* is the agent of change. *Art-Based Group Therapy* is not an adjunct guide. As Moon explains, "It is the unique qualities of art-based group work that I want to examine in this text, in an effort to describe theories and methods that are indigenous to art therapy, rather than adaptations from other helping disciplines."

The following pages will undoubtedly benefit students, practitioners, and educators alike. With this book as a guide, art therapy students may be more empowered to enter into the uncertain terrains of their practica grounded in a theory soundly based in their area of study. Practitioners will no doubt be encouraged, validated, and inspired to continue their work. Educators can employ the twelve principles, as they teach the basic theories and applications of group dynamics and processes. *Art-Based Group Therapy* not only aids in the direct applications of the classroom-learning environment, but does so in a way that underscores the message that art therapy is valued, independent, and self-sustaining.

While this text offers practical advice and provides tools for group art therapy leaders, it is much more than a list of stages, steps, or directives. This book explains, describes, and evokes the *experience* of group art therapy practice. Through the author's effective use of storytelling, the reader encounters the group art therapy experience, transcending the case vignette and didactic instruction. A recipient of the Honorary Life Member Award of the American Art Therapy Association and author of a number of books on art therapy, Moon shares his wisdom and experience in a direct, personal, and authentic manner. He is a passionate advocate for the field and a believer in the power of images. Through his personal disclosures and vivid descriptions of amalgamated clinical situations, the reader is invited into art therapy sessions and given access to the mind, the heart, and the soul of the therapist.

That Moon is able to shape a highly theoretical model into such a personal narrative is an art in and of itself. His invitation to observe both the successes and the struggles of his work (to both show and to tell) models his statement that "Personal meaning can only be found in the context of relationships with others." Reading *Art-Based Group Therapy*, as with all of Moon's works, is an act of engaging in a relationship. Via the shared experience of working with others, readers will find an increased sense of value and meaning in both their current and previous group work. While there is pain, hardship, and uncertainty outlined in these pages, there is also a reassuring comfort in the eloquent explanations and examples of how art heals.

As art therapy continues to work toward gaining recognition and establishing its identity, advocates and practitioners must continually explain, evaluate, and communicate what they do. Moon succeeds in establishing a framework that allows art therapists to communicate the value of their work in a language that is unique to art therapy. Within you will find a specific way of thinking about the diverse gifts of art making applied in the context of creating with others. Bruce Moon has provided the two-by-fours; may this book inspire and empower you to design and build. Like the aforementioned adolescent art therapy group, as the profession of art therapy expands, we are going to need a bigger table and a solid structure within which to house it.

Chris Belkofer, ATR, LCPC

References

Corey, M., Corey, G., & Corey, C. (2008). *Groups: Process and practice* (8th ed.). Belmont, CA: Thompson Brooks/Cole.

Siegel, D. J. (1999). *The developing mind: How relationships and the brain interact to shape who we are.* New York, NY: Guilford Press.

Yalom, I. (2005). *The theory and practice of group psychotherapy* (5th ed.). New York, NY: Basic Books.

INTRODUCTION

A t 10 a.m. in the morning, on September 16 th, 1974, I entered the creative arts building at Harding Psychiatric Hospital in Worthington, Ohio, to participate in my first art-based therapy group. In the ensuing 22 years I led, or co-led, between 10 and 15 art therapy groups per week at the hospital. There were inpatient groups of adults suffering from a wide range of psychiatric disorders. There were groups consisting of hospitalized adolescents, some exclusively boys' groups, some girls' groups, and others that were mixed-gender groups. There were groups of clients from the hospital's outpatient programs, and groups comprised of private practice clients. Finally, there was an on-going group of ever-changing art therapy graduate students that met once a week for over 20 years.

In all of these groups, I have been equally concerned with the processes of making images and objects and responding to them in the company of others. The separation of process and product, a common phenomenon in art therapy that I have addressed in other writings, is for me a theoretical, methodological, and artistic impossibility. In art-based group work processes and products are inextricably connected —two sides of the same coin—and both are necessary partners in self-expression.

The methods of interacting with group members and the artworks they create that are described throughout this book have helped me to realize the unique qualities of art-based therapy experiences. I respond to clients' visual artworks with conversation, painting, bodily gestures, sounds, spontaneous performances, and other forms of creative expression that encourage clients to create in response to my responses. In this text I want to examine the unique qualities of art-based group work in an effort to describe theories and methods that are indigenous to art therapy, rather than adaptations from other helping disciplines.

In 1996 I left Harding Hospital to assume the position of director of the graduate art therapy program at Marywood University in Scranton, Pennsylvania. In that setting I taught and led art therapy group process classes for five years. In 2001 I became the director of the graduate art therapy program at Mount Mary College in Milwaukee, Wisconsin, where again I teach art-based group process courses. Over the last few years I have co-led art therapy groups in a residential treatment facility with adolescent males who have committed a sexual offense.

All of these experiences add up to somewhere in the neighborhood of 30,000 hours spent creating art in the company of clients and students in art therapy groups. This book has been a long time coming. The ideas presented herein have developed slowly, subtly, and gently over the past 35 years. They have whispered to me in the voices of clients and students I have worked with, and for a long time I tried to ignore their voices. I did not want to hear them, nor did I want to commit myself to articulating these ideas for fear of the difficulties I might encounter in attempting to express in words the concepts and experiences that have so often left me speechless. Things happen with and for people in art therapy groups that really are almost magical. It is hard to capture such profound experiences in words alone.

In the aforementioned hours in art therapy groups I have worked with people suffering emotional, behavioral, and mental maladies. Together we have drawn pictures, pushed paint, sculpted, assembled found objects, written poetry, performed dramatic enactments, and made music that expressed feelings and ideas that were beyond words.

Writing this book has been a daunting task. There are, after all, a number of art therapy books that focus on group work (Hanes, 1982; Liebmann, 1998; McNeilly, 2006; Riley, 2001; Skaife & Huet, 1998; Steinbach, 1997; Waller, 1993), and of course there are the classic group therapy texts (Corey, Corey, & Corey, 2008; Rutan, Stone, & Shay, 2007; Yalom, 2005). It is a fair question to ask, "What do I have to offer to the literature of art therapy group work that is different, unique, or needed?" Perhaps an answer to this question is foreshadowed by the title *Art-Based Group Therapy: Theory and Practice*, which expresses my desire to explore the central role that art can play, and I will argue should play, in art therapists' group work. Hence, although this book makes reference to the previously mentioned works, I will offer ideas that have evolved over the years in the hope that my discussions will encourage readers to reconsider the importance of art processes and products in art therapy groups.

The heart and soul of art therapists' work is beyond the scope of precise verbal description, and I am convinced that the greatest validation of art therapy comes in the form of anecdotal testimony from clients. Such evidence is best conveyed in creative narratives that are primarily artistic expressions. I believe that in order to effectively lead art therapy groups one must have faith in the healing and transformative qualities of art processes and products, especially those made in the company of others. I am not opposed to narrative and verbal descriptions—the stories associated with clients' artworks—but I have found that client-artist's understandings of their images can be greatly enhanced by imaginative responses that enable artists to establish deeper emotional and physical relationships to their work, albeit less intellectualized. To paraphrase Paul Simon, "Maybe we think too much." When clients engage all of the senses in cooperation with the mind, they often experience restoration and healing that cannot easily be put into words accessed alone.

Beginnings

Much has written about art therapy groups from the perspective of group therapy and group psychotherapy theory. An example of this is seen in Riley's (2001) conclusion to the first chapter of her book *Group Process Made Visible*:

> Earlier in this chapter 10 themes were quoted from Corey (1990). These 10 themes can serve as the underlying foundation of the art directives. Each emergent theme can translate into a tangible product and provide a record for the growth of the group. (p. 31)

In my view, basing art directives on psychological constructs approaches an understanding of art therapy group work from the wrong direction. I am convinced that too little attention has been given to the essential healing power of art-based approaches to group work, and I hope that this book will remedy that deficiency. I do not intend to disparage other approaches to art therapy group work, but rather hope to add my voice to an evolving dialogue regarding the therapeutic value of art created in community.

The history of art-based group therapy, as discussed in art therapy literature (Riley, 2001; Skaife & Huet, 1998; Waller, 1993), has traditionally been linked to the development of verbal group psychotherapy. As is the case with all art therapy theory, however, there are two primary roots that deserve attention: *psychotherapy* and *art.* Unfortunately, the *art* root has garnered very little attention in relation to the history of art-based group therapy. I would argue that artists have been working in groups considerably longer than psychotherapists have. For example, the earliest known European cave paintings date to 32,000 years ago. Although the purpose of the Paleolithic cave paintings cannot be precisely known, evidence suggests that they were not merely adornments of living areas because the caves in which they have been found show no signs of ongoing human habitation. Some theorists have suggested that they may have been a way of communicating, whereas others ascribe to them ritual or ceremonial purposes. It is not a great leap to imagine that the process of painting held some innate therapeutic benefit for the paintings' creators. Thus one can argue that the history of art-based group work significantly predates the evolution of group psychotherapy.

Another prominent example of artists working together can be seen in the career of Vincent van Gogh (Meier-Graefe, 1987). In 1886 in Paris, van Gogh studied at Fernand Cormon's studio. He participated in the circle of the British-Australian artist John Peter Russell, and met fellow students Émile Bernard, Louis Anquetin, and Henri de Toulouse-Lautrec. The group used to meet at the paint store run by Julien "Père" Tanguy, which was also frequented by Paul Cézanne. No doubt these group meetings provided much needed support, challenge, and inspiration to van Gogh and his contemporaries.

Another example of artists working together in groups is the Art Students League. Founded by and for artists over 130 years ago, the underlying principles of the league have remained basically unchanged. The beliefs that artistic and creativity activity is important, that artists who devote their lives to art are worthy of deep respect, and that there is profound value in educating students in the process of making art, remain the heart of the league's mission. The league was dedicated to encouraging a spirit of unselfishness among its members, and "sympathy and practical assistance (if need be) in time of sickness and trouble" (Steiner, 1999, p. 30).

Of course, cave painters, expressionists, and founders of the Art Students League would not have described their endeavors as being therapeutic in nature, but it is arguable that these, and many other examples of artists sharing space, working collaboratively, and providing support and nurturance to one another, are as much the ancestors of art-based therapy groups as are the early pioneers of group psychotherapy.

Group therapy in the United States can be traced back to the late nineteenth and early twentieth centuries, when millions of people immigrated to America. Most of these immigrants became residents of large cities, and organizations such as Hull House in Chicago were founded to assist them in adjusting to life in the United States. Known as settlement houses, these agencies helped immigrant groups apply pressure for better housing, working conditions, and recreational facilities. These early social work groups valued group participation, the democratic process, and personal growth.

The originators of group psychotherapy in the United States were Joseph H. Pratt, Trigant Burrow, and Paul Schilder, all of whom were active and working in the first half of the twentieth century. For example, in 1905, Pratt formed groups made up of underprivileged patients suffering from a common illness—tuberculosis. Pratt believed that these patients could provide mutual support and assistance to one another. Like settlement houses, his early groups were another forerunner of group therapy.

After World War II, Jacob Moreno, Samuel Slavson, Hyman Spotnitz, Irvin Yalom, and Lou Ormont further developed approaches to group psychotherapy and principles of practice. In particular, Yalom's (2005) approach to group therapy has been very influential in the United States and across the world, as a result of his classic text, *The Theory and Practice of Group Psychotherapy.*

Group psychotherapy in Britain initially developed when pioneers S. H. Foulkes and Wilfred Bion used group therapy as an approach to treating soldiers' combat fatigue in World War II. Foulkes and Bion, both psychoanalysts, incorporated analytic principles into group therapy by recognizing that transference can arise not only between group members and the therapist but also among group members. In addition, the psychoanalytic notion of the unconscious was extended through a theory of a group unconscious, in which the unconscious processes of group members could be acted out in the form of irrational processes in group sessions. Foulkes developed the model known as *group analysis*, whereas Bion was instrumental in the development of group therapy at the Tavistock Clinic in London.

Some early psychoanalysts, especially Alfred Adler, a student of Sigmund Freud, believed that many individual problems were social in origin. In the 1930s Adler encouraged his patients to meet in groups to provide mutual support. At around the same time, social work groups began forming in mental hospitals, child guidance clinics, prisons, and public assistance agencies. A contemporary descendant of these groups is today's support group, in which people with a common problem come together, without a leader or therapist, to help each other solve a common problem. Groups such as Alcoholics Anonymous, Narcotics Anonymous, and Gamblers Anonymous are examples of such groups.

Contemporary Practices

Perhaps more than ever before, today's art therapists are being encouraged to apply their knowledge base to the development of strategies for community building, and art-based approaches to preventing and treating emotional problems. In many settings, individual counseling or psychotherapy is no longer financially feasible. Art-based group therapy allows art therapists to work with many more clients than would be possible in individual sessions. Moreover, art-based group process also has unique qualities that can often serve as the treatment of choice for many clients.

Art-based group processes can be used to enhance participants' sense of community, augment educational endeavors, promote wellness, prevent emotional difficulties, and treat psychological problems. Some art therapy groups may be used to foster coping skills, whereas other groups are intended to promote changes in the ways group members behave and express feelings. Art-based groups may be used in any setting where human well-being is the focus. Art-based approaches may be used with a variety of clients for a host of purposes. In a residential treatment facility for adolescents with behavioral problems, for example, groups can be designed to help clients express feelings appropriately, enhance self-esteem, and develop healthy interpersonal relating skills.

In a psychiatric hospital, art-based groups may focus on helping members clarify and express feelings about problematic issues, aiding in diagnosis, or preparing participants for discharge. Recreational art groups and art groups focused on particular psychological issues such as addictions, trauma, or family conflicts are often found in such settings. In community arts agencies, art-based groups may focus on participants' personal growth or the enrichment of their interpersonal relationships.

In summary, art-based group therapy can help group members achieve nearly any desired outcome. Art-based groups are particularly effective because they allow members to express feelings and relate to others in ways that are not dependent upon the capacity to articulate. Groups also encourage members to practice expressive and interpersonal skills within the group and in their everyday interactions outside of the group. Furthermore, group members benefit from the responses, feedback, and insights they receive regarding their artworks, and from their interactions with peers and the art group leader. Art-based groups offer therapists multiple opportunities for modeling appropriate artistic and interpersonal expression, as well as opportunities for helping clients learn new ways to cope with problems through artistic expression and by observing and interacting with others.

Leaders of art-based therapy groups use nonverbal and verbal techniques along with structured and unstructured artistic exercises. The fundamental roles of the leader are to promote artistic self-expression, facilitate artistic responses, promote interaction among the members of the group, help members to take creative and expressive risks and grow with one another, help them explore and "own" their images, and help them relate to the art therapist.

Ultimately, group members must decide what their goals are and how best to pursue them. The following are some underlying goals that frequently are shared by members of art-based groups:

- Use artistic activity as a means of self-expression
- Recognize the things they have in common with one another and develop awareness of the universal aspects of their difficulties
- Use artistic activity as a way of dealing with emotional issues and as a means to resolve interpersonal conflicts
- Increase self-worth and alter self-concepts
- Use artistic activity as a way of responding to others and expressing compassion for others
- Use art making as a way to clarify feelings and values

Art-based therapy groups have a number of advantages over approaches that rely entirely on verbal interaction. One advantage is that art making is *metaverbal*; that is to say, creative processes and the images that emerge from them are beyond words. Of course, art products can be talked about, but verbalization is not regarded as the primary mode of communication; rather, it serves to validate the messages conveyed in art processes and products. Another advantage is that artistic expression is an inherently healthy process that naturally promotes a sense of satisfaction and improves self-esteem. Art making also provides a means for group members to create symbolic portraits of significant people and events in their lives and to make objects that represent important feelings and thoughts. Art products form a visible record of individual and group process. Whereas words are spoken and then they are gone, artworks remain and can be returned to time and again. Finally, making art in the company of others creates a sense of community and positive energy that is conducive to healing.

I want to emphasize that art-based group therapy is not simply a process of inserting art media and techniques into a verbal therapy group experience. The discipline of leading art-based groups is one of staying with the artistic expressions, trusting that they carry wisdom that cannot always—and perhaps should not—be reduced to the confines of language. I do not discourage spontaneous verbal associations to artworks created in the groups I lead, but when these occur, I recognize them as projections and subjective expressions of feelings and do not dwell upon them exclusively. In my experience, interpretive discussions of images inevitably lead groups away from the artworks themselves and into a more intellectualized form of verbal group therapy. Archetypal psychologist James Hillman (1989) urged practitioners to stick with the image, but I emphasize sticking with the whole range of visual, poetic, physical, and performance expressions that group members create.

Writing *Art-Based Group Therapy: Theory and Practice* was an act of love. The dual loves of art and of my fellow human beings were the sirens that first called me into the art therapy profession. Love has sustained me as the work proceeded. I hope that this book will be an important contribution to group leaders, art therapy students, and the clients they serve.

Bruce L. Moon
Mundelein, Illinois

ACKNOWLEDGMENTS

I am indebted to many people who have contributed to the writing of this book. Thanks go to Bonnie Herbert and Alyssa Miller, graduate assistants at Mount Mary College, for their help in researching the extant art therapy group literature. I am also grateful to those who read, criticized, and encouraged me along the way, especially my editor, Alex Kapitan.

I've been blessed these past 36 years to work with a good number of creative and compassionate colleagues and students at Harding Hospital, Lesley University, Marywood University, Mount Mary College, the Alternative Behavioral Treatment Center, and other colleges and clinical programs. This book would not have been possible without their support.

As always, I am especially indebted to the many members of the art therapy groups I have worked with. Their courage, generosity, resilience, and creativity have been sources of great inspiration and I am thankful to have known them. Their emotional, behavioral, and artistic struggles have motivated me to write and I trust that this book honors them. In many ways *Art-Based Group Therapy* is documentation of the countless lessons clients have taught me.

CONTENTS

ILLUSTRATIONS

ART-BASED GROUP THERAPY

Chapter I

THERAPEUTIC ESSENTIALS OF ART-BASED THERAPY GROUPS

Everything is shaped from something else and in cooperation
with agencies other than ourselves.
                                        –Shaun McNiff (2003, p. 2)

Why Make Art With Others?

A pervasive image associated with artists is that of the lonely and angst-ridden painter toiling in isolation in the studio. An allusion to this image is found in Moon (2009):

> Although I often make art in the company of clients and colleagues, I still regard the experience of looking into the canvas mirror as a solitary process. Since all art is existential, I cannot stand before a blank canvas without experiencing my ultimate aloneness. (p. 224)

As I was thinking about the prevalence of the notion that artists work in isolation I did an Internet search using the keywords "lonely artist." To my surprise there were 13,700,000 results listed. I want to offer a vision of art making in the context of groups that is in contrast to the traditional view of creativity as a singular phenomenon. Given the pervasiveness of the perception that making art is a solitary process, it is reasonable to ask why one should even consider the possibility that making art in the company of others might be therapeutic.

All through human history relationships among individuals have been paramount. Indeed, none of us would survive were it not for the nurturance and support of others. Hence, the capacity to be in relationship to a group–family, friends, or coworkers–is of central importance to mental and emotional well-being. Goldschmidt (as cited in Hamburg, 1963) posited that every person longs for responses from the human environment. This longing may be expressed as a desire for connection, acknowledgment, acceptance, support, positive regard, or mastery.

Perhaps the longing for human connection and response, at least partially, explains why prehistoric humans stained the walls of the caves at Lascaux (Curtis, 2007), and why the Rapa Nui inhabitants of Easter Island (Pelta, 2001) sculpted their monumental statues, and why Frieda Kahlo painted (Herrera, 2002), and why present-day singer-songwriters make music, and why modern dancers move. Acts of creating are invitations to relate. By making things artists take images from within and give them visible form in the world. In profound ways, art making is an act of acknowledgment of the *others* beyond the boundaries of the self. The others are the beholders, members of the audience, the community, and the group.

Few conditions are more distressing to people than loneliness. The foundation of nearly every major approach to psychotherapy is anchored in theories that involve interpersonal relationships. Yalom (2005) stated: "People need people—for initial and continued survival, for socialization, for the pursuit of satisfaction. No one—neither the dying, nor the outcast, nor the mighty—transcends the need for human contact" (p. 24).

Personal meaning can be found only in the context of relationships with others. People create meaning in their lives by being open to another. Creating meaning is not an isolative process. Frankl (1955) pointed out that meaning is found in self-transcendence, not self-actualization. He went so far as to assert, "self-actualization is possible only as a side effect of self-transcendence" (p. 133). Art-based therapy groups provide members with opportunities to form meaningful relationships. Without such relationships there may be little hope for growth or change on the part of the individual client.

The individual self must be transcended for meaning and purpose to be present. "Creating is a participation mystique of many things.... The fertile creator is the one who is sensitive to the expressions and suggestive spirits of environments, things, gestures, relationships, and events" (McNiff, 2001, p. 134). Art is inspired in the territory of interpersonal connection and artists' works are best acknowledged in the domain of relationships. "If we look through something other than ourselves, the object of our contemplation becomes a partner" (p. 134). In art-based therapy groups, clients are able to explore themselves and their relationships by looking through the lens of their partners–peers, art processes, and products.

By creating artworks artists offer views of the world and their unique responses to the world. The community (audience/group) responds to the products of an artist's efforts by attempting to comprehend the uniqueness of the artist. The artist creates, the community responds, the artist makes again, the community attends, and so on. In a broad sense, art making may be considered to always be a group enterprise. "Life is always created from interplay among different participants who make contact, influence one another, exchange their essential natures, merge, and generate new forms" (McNiff, 2003, p. 2). Creating art is a self-transcendent process. The vast majority of artists are very interested in the reactions their work inspires in others. This interest is motivated by the desire for human contact. A central healing quality of art therapy is the capacity to promote the development of relationships. Although some artists state that they must be left alone to do their work, still most intend that someday others will acknowledge their creative work.

> Solitude has a crucial place in creative practice but it is only part of a larger exchange among people, places, and things. Even in our most solitary moments creativity is a group process of interacting forces, images, ideas, and possibilities, all gathering together to make something that is shaped from the unique qualities of their relationship to one another. (McNiff, 2003, p. 2).

Making art is intimately concerned with community and relationship building.

The art therapy groups I've led have invested in me a level of trust to work with the difficulties that group members bring to therapy. Clients draw and paint their images upon the walls of the studio, and through rituals of shared creation we engage in a process of acknowledging the realities of our lives. An almost palpable group energy, artistic contagion, and spirit of support among members draws clients and therapists alike into creative action and social interaction. This is why it is beneficial to people to make art in groups.

In present-day Western society there is a tendency to overvalue immediacy (pleasure now) and undervalue delayed gratification and the hard work that goes into forming deeper relationships and solid emotional foundations (Lasch, 1979; Marin, 1975; B. Moon, 2009; Yalom, 2005). The inflated virtues of rugged individualism are an accepted part of the cultural value system in nearly all segments of society. As a result of this overvaluing of individuality, when significant relationships become difficult and not immediately gratifying, it is as likely that one will simply opt to change partners rather than work to resolve conflicts. It is as if the human components of relationships are viewed as interchangeable parts. This attitude toward relationships was sardonically expressed by a character in a popular Wendy's fast-food restaurant commercial from the 1980s who said, "Parts is parts." This way of viewing relationships is perhaps both the cause and the effect of the marked instability of modern marriages and family life (Rutan & Stone, 2007).

The ability to engage in supportive, loving, and interdependent relationships with others is a significant indicator of psychological health and emotional maturity. Indeed, a fairly accurate gauge of mental health is the degree to which individuals are aware of how important other people are to them.

The clients I have encountered in my art therapy group work over the last 36 years, whether in the psychiatric hospital, residential treatment facility, or private studio, have shared a common struggle to experience and benefit from close and nourishing relationships. This has been true for adolescent and adult clients alike, irrespective of diagnoses, socioeconomic factors, and cognitive abilities. This may be due to the fact that in today's society people have fewer relationships that they can truly count on as they develop their own identities. Rutan and Stone (2007) comment on the transience of modern communal environments such as neighborhoods, extended families, and churches. Each of these has developed porous boundaries and become less cohesive than in past times.

Much of my work in art-based group therapy has focused on helping clients experience the benefits of relationships that form as they engage in creative activities in the presence of one another. In these contexts the problems and expressions of others in the group become the stimulus for genuine and creative personal interaction. One of the most beneficial qualities of artistic activity is its ability to integrate dichotomous forces; "the poison becomes a remedy, and problems are transformed into doorways to new ways of living" (McNiff, 2003, p. 13).

Another common concern of clients, although not as pervasive as the difficulties with relating described above, is the sense that they are "not creative." I would be a much wealthier man if I had a nickel for every time a client has said, "I can't draw." Many people view the arts as the special domain of a select few, as if there is a creativity club to which they do not belong. This fairly common self-judgment, although it initially appears as a roadblock, often serves as the first mile marker on the road to reclaiming creative abilities. Riley (2001) wrote that the group leader "must emphasize that any mark, scribble, or stick figure is acceptable" (p. 7). My response to those who claim that they are not creative is always to divert attention from what they feel they cannot do and refocus on what is unique to them and what they can do. This diversion of attention facilitates a change in clients' general perceptions of creativity and artistic activity. This will be discussed in more depth later in this book.

How Art-Based Therapy Groups Help Clients

How do art-based therapy groups help clients? This is a simple question and yet it may be the most important question addressed in this book. Indeed, the following chapters are an effort to answer this core question. If it can be answered with any sense of certainty, art therapy group leaders will have a critical set of principles from which to plan and guide their approach to group work, and they may also have a theoretical framework that will help translate the phenomena of the art therapy group into language that clinicians from other disciplines can understand. If we can identify and describe the essential roles that art plays in the process of facilitating therapeutic change in people in groups, a coherent foundation will have been constructed from which art therapists may build group treatment plans and strategies.

It has been my experience that the great majority of clients who are referred to art therapy groups, regardless of the nature of the treatment setting, are clients for whom simply talking about their problems has not been sufficiently helpful. Typically they have been or are currently in traditional talk therapy but have not been able to make the desired progress. Charting the course of change in persons participating in art therapy groups is a complex and difficult endeavor comprised of many factors. Change happens in the context of a multilayered weaving of engagement with materials, artistic processes, intra- and interpersonal relationships and experiences. In the art therapy group milieu many important relationships coexist. Clients relate to materials, tools, internal and external images, actions, products, and the art therapist. At the same time the art therapist has relationships with clients, materials, tools, images, actions, and finished products. For clients and art therapists there are multiple sensual experiences that occur simultaneously: tactile, visual, olfactory, and aural. The places where these multidimensional relationships and experiences overlap are the loci of the therapeutic essentials of art-based group therapy.

"In every group the personality and belief systems of the leader will influence the way the group proceeds" (Riley, 2001, pp. 7–8). If a carpenter attempted to describe the entire process of building a house to a layperson, the discussion could be overwhelmingly complicated, and it is likely that the layperson would grasp only bits and pieces of the lesson. However, if the carpenter began by explaining the function of two-by-fours in the construction of walls, the description would be fairly simple to understand. When discussing a complicated topic, it is helpful to begin with the basic building blocks. So let us begin examining the therapeutic qualities of art-based group therapy (the two-by-fours) by exploring 12 therapeutic essentials:

1. Making art in a group setting creates a sense of ritual that provides psychological safety and promotes interpersonal emotional risk-taking.
2. Making art with others is a safe way to express pain, fear, and other difficult feelings.
3. Making art in the presence of others is an expression of hope.
4. Making art is a way to communicate that does not depend solely upon verbalization.
5. Making art in the presence of others reduces isolation and creates a sense of community.
6. Making art in a group setting provides ways to symbolize and express feelings regarding interpersonal relationships.
7. When members of a group make art they create shared experiences in the present.
8. Making art with others fosters a sense of personal and communal empowerment.

9. Making art in a group setting promotes positive regard for the other members of the group.
10. Making art with others is a gratifying and pleasurable experience.
11. Making art in a group setting is an act of self-transcendence.
12. Art making in a group setting often leads to expression of the ultimate concerns of existence.

For our purposes here I will discuss these 12 therapeutic essentials separately, as if they were segregated and distinct. When these factors are at work in art therapy groups, however, they are interdependent and seldom if ever function in isolation from one another. I believe that these therapeutic aspects operate in every type of art therapy group, but their individual influences over the dynamics of particular groups may vary widely depending upon the make up, context, and purposes of a specific group. For example, a group comprised of elderly clients residing in an assisted living facility may be primarily focused on making art in the presence of others in order to reduce isolation and to foster a sense of interconnection and community. The other elements are also at work, but the central focus is on community building. In contrast, a group of adolescent clients struggling with behavioral problems may focus on making art in order to express angry, painful, frightening, and disturbing feelings appropriately. Of course the adolescent clients also benefit from the aspects of empowerment, enhanced self-esteem, positive regard for others, and gratification, but the primary emphasis is placed on safely expressing the difficult feelings that often underlie behavioral problems.

It is also likely that, at any given moment in the life of a group, different combinations of the therapeutic essentials may influence individual members of the same group. As Yalom (2005) noted, "Any given experience may be important or helpful to some members and inconsequential or even harmful to others" (p. 3).

Chapter II

SAFETY, RITUALS, AND RISK

As we consider the therapeutic essentials of art-based group thera-py it is important to acknowledge a range of procedural and lead-ership approaches. Some art therapy group leaders prescribe particu-lar art directives that all members respond to. Others enlist members in a process of shared decision-making and co-creation of the theme(s) of group sessions. Still other art therapy group leaders adopt an open-ended and nondirective approach to the use of media.· Some groups are highly structured, whereas others are loosely organized. Decisions regarding which approach (directed or non-directed) to use depend on the setting and available resources, as well as the nature and needs of the clients (C. Moon, 2002).

In order for clients to take full advantage of the therapeutic benefits of art-based group therapy, regardless of the art therapist's methods in relation to group structure, there are two key qualities that must be present: emotional safety and anxiety. Members must have a sense that the therapy group is a safe place to creatively explore and express their innermost feelings and thoughts, and to develop relationships. At the same time, clients need to experience some measure of anxiety to motivate them to make changes in their lives.

When clients feel safe they experience the art-based therapy group as a protective shelter in which their anxieties provide the energy needed to promote their desired life changes. One of my graduate stu-dents used the metaphor of a teeter-totter to represent this dynamic. At one end of the teeter-totter is safety, and at the other end is anxiety. The art therapist is the fulcrum. "A perfect balance between the two ends is rare, and in fact, becomes boring fairly quickly. Someone always leans back in order to disrupt the stillness of the balance" (B. Moon, 1998, p. 134). Usually, art therapy group leaders do not need to worry about stimulating clients' anxieties; clients typically bring plenty of anxiety with them. Art therapists do, however, need to attend to establishing the safety of the group.

One way that art therapists create a safe milieu is by establishing group rituals. When I speak of ritual in this context I am referring to the idea that rituals are the central truths of a community translated into symbolic actions. Rituals are enactments of metaphors performed in a set, ordered, and ceremonial way. Ritual actions communicate information and reinforce social cohesion. Riley (2001) suggested that it is helpful for art therapists to introduce rituals in order to help group members form a sense of their uniqueness and to foster group identity. People perform rituals in order to symbolize essential truths of existence (Campbell, 1968; B. Moon, 2009). All societies develop rituals that serve as psychological and/or spiritual indicators of significant milestones in individual's lives. Baptisms, coming-of-age initiations, weddings, divorce ceremonies, and funerals all mark important occasions laden with developmental, psychological, communal, and spiritual meanings.

The ritual of the Eucharist in Christianity, for instance, is the story of Christ's brokenness expressed through the symbolic actions of breaking bread and drinking wine. The metaphoric breaking lends itself to multiple interpretations and understandings of the Eucharistic actions, ranging from a reenactment of a historic event (the Last Supper), to a recapitulation of miraculous transubstantiation, to a dramatization of an existential story about human brokenness, and many other possibilities. "While mythology is a way of telling stories about felt experience that are not literal, ritual is an action that speaks to the mind and heart" (Moore, 1992, p. 225). When the members of an art therapy group make art they transform their individual truths into visual artworks in the company of their peers. "Ritual brings together action and idea into an enactment" (Hillman, 1975, p. 137). Creative activity within the art therapy group milieu does precisely what rituals have done within religious communities for centuries.

There are a number of rituals that I practice when leading art therapy groups. When I worked at the psychiatric hospital, for instance, one very simple ritual I enacted had to do with arriving at the studio or group room well ahead of my clients in order to prepare the space. Being a resident at a psychiatric hospital is nearly always a difficult experience. Admission is often a dramatic and traumatic event that symbolizes the client's feeling that his or her life is out of control. A common underlying theme for many clients is that they have not gotten their psychological or emotional needs met in the outside world. In preparing the group room I make sure that there are ample art supplies and I organize the space, arrange chairs, and sweep the floor. This ritual of preparation is a metaverbal expression of the notion that I can provide some of what clients need. I do not talk about this ritual with group members; it is simply part of our experience of the group.

When it comes time for the group to begin, I make a point of closing the door. The ceremonial closing marks the official beginning of the group and establishes a boundary between those outside and those within. Again, without talking about it, this ritual conveys a sense of protection and creation of a safe space. (It should be noted that occasionally there are some clients for whom closing the door has unsettling associations. In those circumstances other means to assure safety are necessary.)

I address group members by name, establish eye contact, and ask how they are feeling that day. Clients often respond to this by sharing rather superficial pleasantries or saying things like, "I'm fine," "Okay," and so forth. The point here is not to engage in an extended conversation about how clients feel but rather to establish a predictable rhythm to the group experience. I respond to each member by saying, "You are welcome here."

After the ritual of welcoming, the group moves into art-making processes. Sometimes we make art in response to directives that I provide, sometimes clients choose to visually elaborate on the feeling they identified in the opening ritual, and at other times participants simply engage in open-ended art making. Regardless of form, group members can count on the fact that they will participate in art making during our sessions. Depending on the needs and goals of a particular group, there may be time allotted within a session to share the artworks clients have created, or not. Sessions end with a closing ritual process of asking people to say what they are leaving with that day. The closing ritual gives group members the opportunity to mark the transition from the intensity of art making and group interaction to the world outside the studio.

The rituals of preparation, welcoming, art making, sharing, and closing establish a predictable rhythm to art-based group therapy sessions that clients very quickly come to rely on. In order for clients to successfully engage in the hard work of being in therapy it is necessary that they experience the art therapy group as a safe and predictable place. In fact, the predictability of the group is a prominent contributor to its safety. This aspect of art-based group work is, of course, paradoxical because it is utterly impossible to predict what will emerge in the images and artworks that group members create. This is the magic, the beauty, and sometimes the awesome power of creatively opening to our responses to our lives in the company of others. As McNiff (2003) noted: "Creating with others is forever permeated by surprise. We never know how different people will respond to the same experience" (p. 11).

It is important to keep in mind that many clients who attend art-based therapy groups have relationship histories that include significant people in their lives behaving unpredictably. The simple act of the art therapy group leader being punctual and ready to engage in rituals of welcoming is a potent message to group members about the art therapist's commitment to the group. Conversely, if group members have to stand at the door to the studio and wait for a late group leader to arrive, regardless of the reason, that too is a powerful message to the clients.

At the start of art therapy groups I always greet members in the same way: "Welcome to the studio!" This simple phrase, uttered in the first few seconds of our encounter, sets the tone for clients' entry into the studio or group room. My affect conveys a sense of excitement about the work ahead and exudes enthusiasm and genuine pleasure that each participant is a member of the group. This ritual of welcoming is a subtle way to begin to establish the creative contagion that I want the members of the group to experience.

As mentioned earlier, it is important to have the necessary material supplies and tools available and well organized before clients enter the group space. This means that I spend time before sessions making sure that we have what we need, and that I monitor the supplies. If we are beginning to run low on pastels, or tagboard, or paint—whatever—I know that it is time to reorder materials.

When working in a nondirective open studio I always have an "artwork in progress" as an element in the group. My commitment to, and enthusiasm for, artistic expression becomes a compelling unspoken force in the group. Henley (1997) noted, "By working in the presence of clients, the art therapist models important art making behaviors which clients can begin to identify with and incorporate" (p. 190). My artwork provides a vehicle for ritual greetings with group members. Clients will often enter the studio and ask, "What's this about, Bruce?" This gives me the opportunity to model self-exploration and expression in an authentic way with clients.

I also consciously work to develop rituals for the ending of group sessions. Near the end of each session I announce to the group, "Five-minute warning!" And when it is time to prepare for leaving I announce, "Time to clean up." Each of these things, and many more, established patterns give group members a sense that the art therapy group environment is a safe and predictable place. They know in advance what will be expected of them and what they can expect from me. These rituals of safety and predictability establish the boundaries of the group container that holds the surprising, mysterious, and unpredictable contents of the creative process.

Establishing art-based therapy group rituals are not only the domains of group leaders. Group members also design group rituals. Rituals are often developed as a way to impart the history and norms of the group to new members. In this way the group maintains its own culture. For example, several years ago a tradition of using chalk to smudge the cheek of new members on their first day in the group evolved in a group of adolescent girls. The smudging served as a ritual of initiation to that group. Although the original *smudgers* had left the group years earlier, the smudged cheek signified warmth and acceptance of each new member for quite some time. In another example members of an all male group established the tradition that when a member left the group, the peer who had been closest to him would take over the discharged client's workspace and sit in his chair. This ritual honored the client who had left and created a sense of continuity among the remaining members.

The Rituals of Making Art With Others

Although the rituals of preparation, welcoming, sharing, and closing all contribute to the safety and predictability of art therapy groups, the ritual qualities of making art in the company of others are the most important. If we understand rituals to be enactments of essential truths of existence then we know that when members of an art therapy group make art they are engaging in profound self-revelation, even when creating the simplest things. When art therapy group leaders embrace this idea they are able to enact the most fundamental tenet of therapeutic art practice: that positive energy inspires creative activity. One image begets another, and another, and another.

Art-based therapy groups are often comprised of people who do not consider themselves to be creative or artistic. For such clients, artistic expression can lead to feeling exposed and vulnerable, and their creativity is often fragile and easily extinguished. Art therapy group leaders need to exude encouragement and affirmation of clients' creative expressions and consistently look for ways to support artistic activity.

Art-based therapy groups offer many opportunities for reparative experiences. As clients make art in the context of the therapy group they create a social microcosm. Problematic relating skills that have contributed to clients' difficulties almost immediately emerge in the group. In the group setting clients typically display the dysfunctional behaviors that have led them to seek therapy. Maladaptive patterns of relating inevitably are enacted in the group. Art-based therapy groups provide opportunities to repair the trauma of past experiences by transforming maladaptive behavioral reactions into creative working-through activities. Such transformations occur when members feel safe in the group and when there is honest reflection on the images that are made during the session.

One such transformation was seen in the case of J.T., a 20-year-old client who had been remanded to a residential treatment facility by court authorities for evaluation after being arrested and charged with assault. In a pre-group planning meeting with colleagues from the treatment and evaluation team it was predicted that J.T. would use his truculent interactive style as a way to keep others at a safe distance. He entered the group with a surly and aggressive strut that exuded an air of intimidation. The opening ritual of the group was to gather in a circle in the studio where I would check in with each client by asking how he or she was feeling that day. It was not surprising that J.T. made a subtly threatening and disrespectful remark in response to a comment that one of the other group members made. I responded, "J.T., there is no need to be so hostile here. You don't have to be on guard."

He glowered and growled, "I hate this shit. Why'd they make me join this group?"

In a most positive voice I replied, "J.T., that's perfect. The whole point of being in this group is to express yourself, and you certainly did." (It should be noted that my response to J.T. was not what he expected. By responding positively to his verbal expression, albeit a rather hostile expression, I sidestepped his effort to engage me in conflict, and in fact was able to subtly compliment his expressiveness. It is helpful for group leaders to regard art therapy sessions as if they were performance art events, and group members as if they were actors in a dramatic enactment. As I considered J.T.'s hostile behaviors as scenes from a drama I was free to observe and reflect upon the meaning of his performance without becoming counter-therapeutically caught up in the drama itself. It seemed to me that his typical style of interacting was designed to keep him distant from others and to protect him. His apparent need for protection and distance suggested that he had been hurt in the past and I decided that it would not be helpful to react in a challenging way. Rather than confront his behavior, or be put off by it, I responded in a way that would allow me to possibly become his ally rather than his adversary.) Addressing the other members of the group, I said, "In fact that's exactly what we want to do today—make art about something that is on your mind." I turned toward J.T. and said, "You are welcome here, J.T. You've already said that you hate this, so I wonder, if you turned that feeling into a color, what would it be?"

He sniggered, "Shit brown, man. Smeared everywhere."

"Okay then, how about painting it?"

J.T. looked at me suspiciously, but because everyone else in the group was gathering materials and beginning to work, he went along with the assignment. "What do I paint on?"

"There are couple pieces of Masonite in the painting rack that you could use, or if you'd like I could help you build a canvas," I said.

He looked over the options and selected an 18" x 24" piece of Masonite fiberboard. When he went to the paint cabinet, however, he said, "I don't see any brown here."

I replied, "We must be out of brown, but don't worry about that, it is easy to make brown."

He sneered, "I don't know how to make brown." This was an important moment because J.T. had acknowledged that he did not know something, that is that he was not self-sufficient and in control. "I can show you how to make brown, J.T. Let's start with equal amounts of red and green." I handed him a palette and added, "Just scoop out about a silver dollar-sized blob of each color, and then swirl them together."

J.T. appeared skeptical, but he followed the directions and as he mixed together the cadmium red and Hooker's green he was clearly surprised and gratified by his success in creating brown. It is important to note that this kind of interaction would not have been possible in a group setting that relied solely on verbal interactions. In this instance, the art materials served as neutral others, elements in the milieu that helped to divert J.T.'s hostility.

As he finished blending the red and green J.T. said, "Damn, that's alright."

Another group member, Anthony, looked over at J.T.'s brown and joked, "That looks like crap."

J.T. laughed and retorted, "That's what it's supposed to look like, man." He turned to me and asked, "Now what?"

I replied, "Let's use your brown as a background color. Cover the entire board with brown."

After slathering most of the Masonite with his brown paint, J.T. complained, "This isn't covering everything. I can see white flecks showing through."

Betty, a peer of J.T.'s who had kept her distance from him, looked up from her work and said, "If you just touch your brush in a little bit of water it'll help the paint flow better and cover up everything."

J.T. glared at Betty momentarily, but his angry look softened as he said, "Thanks, I'll try that." When the Masonite was completely covered with brown paint he asked, "How's this, man?"

"Yowsa," I said. "That sure is brown." A slight smile almost formed on his angry, bored face. "I wonder what color would look good against that excremental brown?"

He uttered an insolent guffaw. "Whaddya want me to do now?"

"Well, like I said before, let's think of the brown as a background for your painting. If you were going to write something like 'This is shit, I don't want to be here' on that background, what color would you want to use to really get your point across?"

"I don' know, red I guess."

"J.T., I know that writing that on your painting would not go over very well with the staff here, so what kind of line could you make that would express that same feeling?"

"What are you talkin' about?"

I demonstrated. "Pretend there is an imaginary blackboard in front of me. Would it be a line like this—I drew a wavy gentle line in the air in front of me—"or like this?" My air brushstroke became harsh and jagged.

"Like that," he said, as he made a rough and jerky gesture.

"Cool," I said. "Now do that over your brown with red."

When he'd finished his jagged line we looked at his work.

"You know, J.T., as I look at this it seems a little too flat. Your feelings are powerful, aren't they?"

"Yeah, I guess."

"How about adding some orange highlights and black shadows to the red line, just to give it more depth . . . more energy."

And he did.

When it was finished, J.T.'s painting (see Figure 1 & Plate 1) was a simple but powerful expressive image. I said, "I like to think that when we make art everything we make is a partial self-portrait."

J.T. responded, "I'm not sure 'bout that. But I like doing this."

As the session neared its end Anthony commented on J.T.'s painting, "Damn, that looks angry, man!"

J.T. smiled and said, "Yeah, sure as hell."

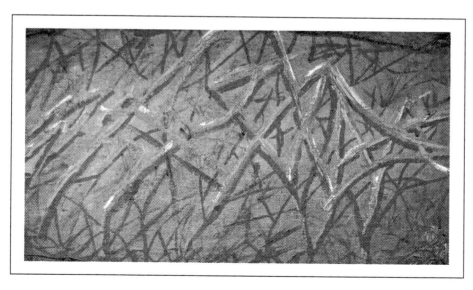

Figure 1. J.T.'s Brown

In subsequent sessions, J.T. painted and drew many feelings. He created images of emptiness, and anger, and the bewilderment he felt regarding a number of painful events from his past. As he entered the group he almost always had an edge of hostile braggadocio, but he would quickly settle into a different way of being in the art therapy group room. Clearly, the supportive interactions with his peers and me, in concert with his engagement with art materials and the expressive content of his images, combined to provide J.T. with reparative emotional experiences.

When J.T. came into the art-based therapy group he expected to fight with me. He expected to use his typical hostile interactive style to turn me into an enemy. By honoring his feelings I avoided his initial interactive assault. The attention that group members and I gave him provided a milieu that was conducive to making art while at the same time being focused on the development of relationships. As J.T. made art in the company of others we created a common ground from which our relationships could grow. I paid attention to his behaviors and interactions as if they were components of a performance art event and this allowed me to look, listen, and respond to his artistic and dramatic communications as a therapeutic ally. Making art in the group setting created a sense of ritual that provided J.T. with psychological safety that promoted self-expression and interpersonal emotional risk-taking.

In art-based group work I see the art therapist's role as one of serving and maintaining the structure of the group, as well as being a holder of the studio space. Although my art-based practice differs from more traditional psychodynamic group psychotherapy approaches, I do not think of it as non-clinical. As McNiff (2004) noted, "There is no irreconcilable split between art and clinical care" (p. 28). The term *clinical* denotes accuracy, paying attention to the needs of others, and authentically responding to people and their creative work.

Perhaps the most fundamental healing quality of art-based group therapy is the sense of ritual that develops naturally as people make art together in the same space. When art therapists are truly able to be present and to hold the structure of the group while at the same time being open to whatever group members need to express, a sense of safety inevitably emerges. Members have often commented to me that they experience a quality of sacredness in our group sessions. That sacred quality is the direct result of the repetitive and ritualistic elements involved in communal art making and the feeling that the studio is an emotionally safe space. The power of creative expression is unleashed when people feel safe, and conversely people feel safe when their efforts to express themselves artistically are nurtured and respected.

Art-based group therapy leaders are responsible for creating a sense of sanctuary in the studio or group room. The art therapist works to shape the culture of the group in ways that embrace creative expression in all of its forms, even when the content of a particular expression may be disturbing. The leader stimulates the creative energy of the group and activates a dynamic interplay among people, images, materials, and the studio space. When the expressive energies of group members are encouraged and responded to in authentic ways, the studio becomes an artistic sanctuary.

J.T.'s uttered desire to "smear shit" was certainly not a pleasant prospect, but by avoiding his invitation to conflict and honoring his underlying expression of anger, I was able to help J.T. align himself with the positive energy of the art-based therapy group. As he became involved with art materials and interactions with his peers and me, he immersed himself in the ritual flow of the group experience. This created an atmosphere of acceptance, authenticity, and healing that is the hallmark of a safe and sacred place.

Every art-based therapy group evolves rituals of beginning, artistic immersion, interpersonal sharing, closure, and termination that provide predictability and safety. Such rituals are enactments of the unwritten rules and norms that support clients' participation and behavior in the group. Group rituals are shaped by the behavior, attitude, and modeling of the art therapy group leader, and by the expectations and needs of group members. The leader is extremely influential in establishing the rituals that shape the culture of the art-based group, and in fact, cannot avoid this function. Rituals constructed in the initial stages of the group have considerable durability. Thus, art therapy group leaders are advised to consider this function very deliberately and with great care.

Chapter III

MAKING ART WITH OTHERS IS
AN EXPRESSION OF HOPE

Hope is an important therapeutic aspect in art-based group therapy. Leaders must have hope for their group members, and clients need hope for themselves. "If there is no hope, there will be no therapeutic progress" (Moon, 2009, p. 154). Hope is an attribute of effective art-based group leaders that lies beneath their beliefs about their clients, themselves, and the basic purposes of group work (Couch & Childers, 1987). Group members need to have faith in the art therapist and in their peers, and group leaders must have faith in the art process, themselves, and the essential goodness and value of each member of the group.

Art therapists ought not expect group members to enter the studio filled with hope. On the contrary, it is much more likely that, at least initially, clients will feel rather hopeless. The art-based group leader's hope, then, must be deep and unyielding. Hope requires faith. Making art in the presence of others is a tangible, yet metaverbal, expression of hope. In a truly profound and perhaps unconscious way, making art is an act of benevolence, a way of giving to the world. To give in this way, one must at some level believe that there is something or someone out there worthy of the gift.

I have seen this principle repeatedly enacted in art-based therapy groups in psychiatric hospitals, residential treatment facilities, and university art therapy studio classes. Members who have been in a group for a while subtly welcome and initiate newcomers, and veterans assure new members that the art-based group process is worthwhile, and, in fact, can be good. Graduate students get past their superficial differences and abandon their competitiveness as they allow themselves to form authentic relationships with one another.

Hope is conveyed artistically, verbally, behaviorally, and metaphorically. One observable expression of this is seen when clients donate finished artworks to the studio or group room. Whenever possible such gifts are displayed on the walls. Images emanate positive energy and stimulate the environment, conveying the powerful unspoken message, "Have faith and hope."

A critical element in creating a studio atmosphere that metaverbally coveys a sense of hope is the group leader's conviction that making art in the company of others is both healthy and healing. Belief in the goodness of communal art making is contagious. This is why art-based group leaders should remain active artists. Faith in the art-making process is nurtured in the group milieu that regards creative self-expression as a declaration of hope.

Julianne's Despair

Julianne was quiet as she entered the art therapy group room. She was 42 years old but looked closer to 60. Her eyes were listless and dull. I knew from the referral summary that she had been married and divorced twice, and that she had a long history of alcoholism. She had a resigned and rather rough appearance.

Julianne had brought herself to the emergency room. She showed up late one evening and told the desk worker that she would either be admitted to the treatment program that night or she might be dead by morning.

As she came into the group room her eyes seemed dispirited, her hair was pulled back in a simple ponytail, she wore no makeup, and her clothes smelled of cigarette smoke. As I was giving her a quick tour of the studio, she paused to look at a painting that hung on one of the walls. The image was a representation of a phoenix rising out of swirling flames.

I said, "That painting was done by one of our group members a few years ago."

Julianne glanced at me warily and asked, "Why is it still here?" There was a hint of distrust and hostility in her voice.

"Well, she could have taken it with her," I said. "But she wanted to leave it here for groups that would come later."

"Why in the world did she do that?" she asked.

"You'd really have to ask her to get all the details, Julianne, but the short answer is that she had a good experience in the group," I said. "She wanted to leave a part of herself behind, to give something to future group members."

She frowned and grumbled, "I can't imagine having a good experience here."

Overhearing this, Andy, an older man who'd been in the group for several sessions, said, "I can."

Julianne turned toward Andy and scoffed, "Did anyone ask you?"

Andy looked up from his work uneasily and said, "No, no one asked. But I overheard you and Bruce. You really asked him an impossible question. How can you expect him to answer? If he told you that people like the group you'd just say that he's lying." Andy looked back toward his artwork and added, "All I can say is that I've been here a couple of weeks, and I've seen this happen a couple a' times. New people come in to the group feeling horrible, and Bruce does his spiel about making art will help. They don't believe him."

"Sounds hard to believe to me," Julianne said.

Andy went back to his work and said, "Well, look at that bird coming up outta the ashes. You never can tall what might happen. One thing I know though, you'll get out of the group whatever you are willing to put into it."

I chimed in, "Andy is right. You'll get what you give in the art group. Now, let's get to work."

It is vital that art group leaders have a resolute conviction that art making in the presence of others is healing. If leaders have faith and trust in the power of the creative process, their faith will be contagious.

Julianne expressed little interest in making art. During the next few sessions she kept herself busy by gathering mosaic tiles, sorting them by color, arranging them in patterns, and ultimately returning them to the jumbled mass of tiles in the storage bin. She would superficially engage in social interactions with her peers and on occasion comment on another group member's artwork, but for the most part Julianne kept her feelings and opinions to herself. I sometimes felt an urge to confront what I perceived to be her lack of meaningful involvement in art activity and her superficial relating style, but something, a hunch perhaps, kept me from doing so. I decided instead to stay focused on my own creative work and to trust that something positive was happening for Julianne, even though I could not easily describe what that was. As an art-based group therapist, I have often experienced moments when I find myself caught between my desire to direct meaningful change in clients' lives and my faith in creative processes and the inherent wisdom that those same clients possess. I have been reminded many times that clients make changes at their own pace, in their own good time, and that their itinerary often has nothing to do with my preplanned schedule.

Julianne had been in the art group for six or seven sessions when, in the midst of a session, I noticed her standing in front of the full-length mirror gently applying tempera paint to her face with her fingers. The left side of her face was nearly covered with alternating black and white horizontal lines. As I watched, she was absorbed in placing fingertip-sized daubs of color to the right side. I approached quietly and exclaimed "Yowsa, Julianne, that is quite a mask!"

She glanced at me in the mirror, but did not turn my way. "This is no mask, Bruce." For a few moments neither of us spoke as she continued to apply paint.

Joanne, another member of the group, was heading toward the sink to rinse out her brushes. She paused and said, "Looks like you are getting ready for war!"

Julianne grimaced, but she did not respond. She continued to apply paint until the right side of her face resembled an impressionist's interpretation of a kaleidoscope.

Near the end of the session the members of the group were seated in a circle of chairs to share what they had created that day. When her turn came to talk about her work, Julianne reached into a bucket of warm water that she had placed at her feet, removed a sponge, and proceeded to cleanse her face. Her movements were slow and methodical; she did not hurry.

The other members of the group appeared to be captivated by her simple, repetitive motions, and as the paint was washed away and Julianne's natural skin revealed, I could see tears glistening in the eyes of her peers. When she had finished the room was heavy with reverential silence. After several moments, Joanne spoke, "I don't really know what that was all about, Jul', but it was beautiful."

Andy sighed, "Amen."

For a minute or so no one said a word, but several group members let tears slide down their cheeks.

Acceptance of the realities we face is essential if we are to transform negative experiences into affirmations of life. Hope occurs when we are open to the creative impulses that move through us. In hindsight, it is possible to imagine that Julianne's initial process of sorting and arranging tiles was a self-designed warm-up exercise. By making order out of small, random bits and pieces she flexed and stretched her emotional muscles and at the same time opened herself to the energies of the colors and shapes of mosaic tiles. When she was ready, she moved to the canvas of her own body. As McNiff (2004) noted:

> Art therapy is a discipline that encourages us to create from the difficult places in life, and the skilled art therapist helps us to openly engage the most challenging conditions with a confidence that the creative process will transform conflicts into something new. (p. 218)

My work with people in art-based therapy groups has convinced me that clients' pain, along with their artistic activity, are indispensable partners in the process of building hope. Dark and troubling aspects of life are welcomed into the studio or group room and are allowed to make their way toward transformative healing. As Joanne indicated in the vignette above, she didn't know the details of Julianne's life, nor did she know exactly what Julianne was trying to express, "but it was beautiful."

I want to emphasize here how important it was that I did not attempt to control or direct Julianne's creative process. Although I was tempted to do so, I was able to let go of my need to be in charge and simply trust that something good would come out of her work even though I could not predict the outcome of her creative process. By letting go of my need to control the pace of Julianne's work in the group, she was enabled to go with the flow of her own creative process and find a way to express and enact important themes from her life. I did not get in her way. In doing so she was able to express feelings and also capture the compassionate sympathies of her peers in the group, and thus take us all outside of ourselves and connect us to the creative and hopeful energy that moves through life. This is why art therapists must remain artistically active, because it is in the process of creating our own art that such faith and hope is nurtured.

Chapter IV

MORE THAN TALKING CURES

The disciplines of counseling and psychotherapy have remained true to their roots as "talking cures." This is why the vast majority of literature concerning group therapy emphasizes verbal interaction as, the primary mode of operation. This emphasis is anchored in a bias toward linear discourse that suggests that every issue should be talked about. Expressing this bias, a counselor colleague of mine has gone so far as to say that if a problem cannot be talked about, it cannot be resolved. Art therapists, however, know that there are many people in the world who cannot or will not express their feelings verbally.

When I worked in a psychiatric hospital, I was often referred child and adolescent clients who were survivors of physical and/or sexual abuse. Working with these clients helped me understand that not every feeling can be put into words. The young children did not have the vocabulary to express how they felt about the horrible things that had happened to them. Adolescent clients were often so angry with the adult perpetrators that the last thing they were going to do was share their feelings with other adults. Yet in both instances the children and teenagers had feelings that were wreaking havoc on their lives and they desperately needed to find ways to express themselves and be understood.

In art-based group therapy we often witness creative expressions of feelings that are beyond the communicative abilities of conventional speech. The linear language of logical conversation cannot convey the subtle nuances of artistic expression, nor even the most basic qualities of a creative enactment. These aspects of creative experience have not been included in traditional group psychotherapy theory and discourse.

29

It can be argued that the most important aspects of art-based group therapy happen in the interactions among the client, media, image, artistic processes, and other members of the group, and that group leaders' primary tasks are to provide an environment that facilitates these interactions.

The metaverbal nature of art therapy is easy to comprehend in relation to clients' individual work in the art therapy studio. It is harder to understand in relation to art-based group therapy because of the verbal discussion that occurs in the context of group work. In my art groups, clients talk about their creations. The pictures, objects, lines, shapes, movements, sounds, and colors transmit feelings and energies that inspire discussion among group members. Talking is an important part of our interactions with artworks and peers, but it is only one way of responding. Over the years I have seen that when spoken language is the only way we interact with our artwork or the works of others, then we are becoming too constrained in our relationships.

When I talk with graduate students about the principle of metaverbal interaction in art-based group courses, they often raise questions regarding the practical application of this principle. My response to their questions is that the core of the therapeutic work that occurs in art-based group therapy has been done before clients say anything about their creative expressions. Talking about the creative process and finished artworks is the icing on the cake. The main course of the therapeutic meal takes place among clients, media, process, and product. The essence of art therapy group work is beyond the expressive capacity of spoken words. This is not to disparage verbalization, but rather to venerate actions, images, and creative metaverbal interactions.

In light of the discussion of the metaverbal nature of art-based group therapy, one may wonder why group leaders would ever talk. The answer to that question is that human beings are naturally talkative creatures. Talking about images, paintings, drawings, and other art forms offers psychological safety and security for group members. Talking about artistic processes and products provides an opportunity to create emotional distance from the powerful feelings often evoked through the work.

For example, in the case of a young woman displaying anxiety and features of post-traumatic stress disorder, it was helpful to encourage her to talk about images she created of the sexual abuse she had endured. It was helpful to her to be assured by members of the group that children are in no position to ward off such inappropriate sexual behaviors on the part of adult authority figures. One of her peers exclaimed, "It wasn't your fault, Anne, you are guilty of nothing. You have a right to be angry." These words offered Anne consolation as she wrestled with painful events from her past.

In contrast is the case of a middle-aged businessman who came to a group seeking treatment for depression. It became apparent that in addition to being clinically depressed, he had been drinking excessively. On the surface he was charming, yet he was also subtly unreliable. He was adept at using his facile social skills to keep himself a safe distance from others in the group.

During one session, in response to the drawing task "Portray the animal in your head and the animal in your gut," he depicted a Bambi-like deer in his head and a shark in his belly. When his turn came to talk about his images, he launched into a comedic monologue. Everyone in the group was laughing except me. I said nothing.

When it became evident that I was not going along with his effort to entertain the group, he looked at me and asked, "What's the matter?"

I opened my mouth as if about to speak, but remained silent.

He raised his voice, "Is there a problem?"

I quietly said, "It must be hard."

Looking toward his peers with mixed annoyance and desperation, he jeered, "I don't get it."

Again I said, "It must be hard."

"What are you talking about? What must be hard?" he asked.

I replied, "It must be hard carrying a shark around inside."

In this interaction I used my words carefully to validate the potential meanings expressed in this client's artwork. It seemed apparent that, at a metaverbal level, he had begun to struggle with the incongruity of his mild and sociable (Bambi) exterior, and the frightening inner feelings characterized by the shark image.

In responding to group members' artworks I try to use spoken words in ways that amplify the sensual experience of the artworks, and I encourage clients to use their imaginations in responding to one another. The following is an example of how I used imaginal dialogue in an art-based group session in which members had created images of "a safe place."

Addressing Marianne, a client who'd portrayed a farmhouse in an open prairie setting, I said, "When I look at your painting I can almost hear the wind rustling against the house." Then I made a low whooshing sound, "Whoooooooo."

Marianne closed her eyes and replied, "I can almost feel it on my face."

I went on, "Something about your painting reminds me of a warm summer day."

Erin, another group member, reacted to my comment by remarking, "I think it looks cold."

I responded to Erin, "If it's cold, do you think it would be autumn or winter?"

Marianne interjected, "fall is a season of letting go."

Another member, Ellen, asked, "What would you be letting go of?"

Marianne paused and as she thought about how to respond to Ellen's question, her hands, which had been clenched, gently opened. She said, "I'm not sure."

I commented, "A moment ago your hands opened. It was a beautiful gesture. Could you do it again?"

Marianne made a fist with her right hand and then opened it quickly.

"Try to do it more slowly," I urged, "Get into how it feels to open."

She pulled her right hand into a fist again, and then relaxed. I suggested that she try with both hands. Again, Marianne clenched her fists, then slowly and gracefully opened them.

I responded, "There was something different that time. You seemed to move more gently."

Marianne said, "Ellen asked what I'm letting go of, and when I did that it felt like I had a handful of sand, or dust. When I opened my hands the wind blew the dust away."

I replied, "If you imagine yourself in this place, with the wind blowing the dust from your hands, where would you be?"

She looked at her painting and said, "I'd be standing on the porch, looking out at the vastness of it all."

Erin commented, "It looks like a lonely place."

Ellen said, "Reminds me of that old Kansas song . . . 'Just a drop of water in an endless sea.' She hummed, "All we are is dust in the wind."

In this brief exchange, rather than relying on interrogative questions, the group used imaginal and sensual words. *Wind, warm, fall, winter, dust,* and *letting* go are words that invited imaginative thinking and interaction. By using language in this way the group members entered into sensual and image-based dialogue with one another. The intent of such conversations is not to categorize or label artworks or clients, but rather to become immersed in the creative flow and deepen our relationships and understandings of each other.

I want to be clear about this point: The crucial therapeutic work in the art-based therapy group sessions takes place among artists, media, processes, and images, in the presence of the group leader. Words are used to deepen involvement with artworks, facilitate interactions, validate expressions, and affirm and encourage creative work. Group leaders know that there are many people who cannot or will not express their feelings verbally. Such people need art-based groups to provide more than talking cures.

Chapter V

CREATING COMMUNITY

As an existentialist, I believe that one of the underlying truths of human existence is that we are ultimately alone. In a sense, our aloneness forces us to be responsible for our lives; nobody can live them for us. Jim Lantz (personal communication, November, 1993) used the metaphor of birth to describe the tension between aloneness and connection:

> The child is cast out from the warmth of symbiosis with the mother. Within a few seconds, the baby is laid back on the mother's belly. That is the rest of our lives, negotiating our separateness and our connection to others.

As I have considered Lantz's words over the years I have come to see that regardless of how intimate we become with one another, the ultimate separation is almost impossible to bridge, and yet between mother and child there is a connection that defies explanation. This quality of existence stimulates yearnings for meaningful relationships, self-reliance, and a sense community.

Making art in the presence of others reduces isolation and creates a sense of connection. I have seen this therapeutic principle at work in many diverse settings: psychiatric hospitals, cancer counseling centers, community counseling agencies, prisons, university classrooms, hotel meeting rooms and conference sites, and nursing homes.

In a residential treatment center for adolescent boys I worked with a group from a unit devoted to caring for clients who had been remanded to the facility by the juvenile court system. The group consisted of four young men, each of whom had histories that included multiple placements in the homes of relatives, foster homes, psychiatric hospitals, and other social service agencies. Each was a ward of the state's Department of Child and Family Services. One client, Shawn, was Caucasian. Francisco was Latino, and Antoine and Devon were African American.

Each of these boys had suffered so many abandonments and so many betrayals of their trust that they had assumed guarded, detached, and reflexively hostile ways of being in the world. In the early days of our group, they had little or no interest in one another, and no use for me. They were sullen, defensive, and inaccessible, and they had every right to be so.

When they entered the studio that first day I was working on a painting. I'd covered most of the canvas with black paint. A staff member introduced us and then left. I said, "Welcome to the studio. We make art here." Shawn immediately headed for a place at a table in the far corner of the room, as far away from me as possible. Francisco took up a position by the bank of windows and stared out at the winter landscape. Antoine moved toward the boom box and sorted through a stack of CDs. Devon moved to a stool across the table from me. An overhead view of their movements would have been reminiscent of magnetically charged particles repelling one another; each finding a separate place outside the sphere of influence of the others. I continued to paint, but said, "Take a look around and see what you would like to do. Again, you are welcome here."

After a few moments had passed, I stepped away from my painting and addressed Devon, inquiring, "You like art?"

He nodded, "Taggin'."

I continued painting, using black to get rid of the white gesso.

Antoine asked, "Music okay?"

"Sure." I replied.

Wyclef Jean's "Fast Car" filled the room.

Shawn put his head down on the table and closed his eyes. Antoine's hands slapped rhythms on his legs. Francisco's eyes took in barren trees and snowdrifts. Devon asked, "Wha' you doin'?"

"I had a painting professor in college who always said the most important thing was to get rid of the white as quick as possible."

Devon laughed, "I know that feeling!"

Paul Simon's cameo contribution to "Fast Car" resonated in the spaces between the five of us.

"Isn't that something?" I queried. No one responded. I went on, "I mean, Paul Simon's an old white guy, but there he is singing right along with Wyclef Jean."

Another minute or two passed, and I asked, "Anybody have questions about this group, or anything you want to ask me?"

Devon shook his head and said, "Nah, staff told us about it."

Francisco turned away from the windows and asked, "What do I have to do to get out of this?"

"Yowsa, Francisco, I've never been asked that before. I guess you don't have to do anything."

His dark eyes riveted me. "What's that mean, I don' have to do anything?"

Before I could respond to Francisco, Shawn feigned a loud snore and everyone laughed. Devon asked "I like to work big . . . use paint markers. That all right?"

"Sure. Do you know where things are?"

Devon gathered materials, selecting a 3 feet by 2 feet sheet of tagboard, an assortment of wide-edged markers, and began to work. Wyclef Jean's music provided a sound track for this first session. There was little conversation as I painted, Devon tagged, Shawn pretended to sleep, Francisco stared out the window, and Antoine played air drums.

Although it may not sound like much was happening in the way of group interaction, it was significant that these damaged and distrustful boys stayed in the studio. The room, maybe 20 feet by 12 feet, held their separateness, and for a 90-minute session they were all in the same place at the same time; separate, but together.

When I was a kid I loved TV westerns: "Gunsmoke," "Wyatt Earp," "The Rifleman," "Batt Masterson," "Sugarfoot," "Cheyenne," "Have Gun Will Travel" . . . and so on. A common element in those programs was the inevitable gunfight scene. The hero walked down the middle of an empty and dusty street. The villain emerged from the saloon and made his way into the street. The stood face to face—maybe 20 feet apart (B. Moon, 2009, p. 93).

I surely hoped that our encounter would not be harmful to any member of the group, but although we did not have guns, it was evident that Devon, Shawn, Antoine, and Francisco were checking me out, wondering how I would react to them.

Over the next four or five weeks our group sessions proceeded in much the same way: Devon drawing, Antoine keeping the beat, Shawn withdrawn, and Francisco watching the weather outside. No one said very much, but we continued to gather in the studio on

Tuesday afternoons. Nobody skipped a session, and nobody refused to attend. I couldn't seem to find a direction for my painting. I would start one image, get frustrated, and cover it over with black. At one point Devon asked, "How many layers you gonna put on that, Dr. Bruce?"

I shook my head. "I'm not sure, Devon. Something just isn't working with this. But that's the beauty of painting. Anything that can be painted once can be painted twice. You make a mistake, you just paint over it. Sorta' like life. You make a mistake, you gotta back up and try things a different way."

Shawn turned his head my direction and said, "It's not that easy, Dr. Bruce. Some mistakes can't be painted over."

On the CD player Keb Mo sang the chorus from Nick Lowe's ("What's So Funny 'Bout) Peace, Love and Understanding," and there was a heaviness in the air.

Prior to the next session, I decided to shift my focus away from the two-dimensional painting I'd been working on to a three-dimensional project representing the five of us. I found an old wooden bushel basket in my garage and brought it with me to the group. When the boys were escorted to the studio I was hunched over my basket, immersed in the process of covering it with gesso. I said, "Welcome to the studio," and we exchanged minimalist greetings.

As Francisco headed for the windows he asked, "Where's your black painting, Dr. Bruce?"

I straightened and said, "It's over in the painting rack. I thought a lot about our conversation last week about making mistakes and backing up. You guys inspired me to go a different direction and try something new."

Antoine sarcastically commented, "We inspired you to paint that damn basket white! How good is that!"

Without responding to his sardonic tone, I replied, "Yes, indeed you did. Wait till you see how this is going to turn out." I returned to coating the basket.

Shawn spoke up. "Remember back when you said that ol' white guy singing with Wyclef was cool?"

"Paul Simon, you mean. Sure."

"I thought about it," he said. "The staff took us to the library last week and I found another one like that."

"Who'd you find?" I asked.

Shawn pulled *Riding With the King,* a CD featuring collaborations between B. B. King and Eric Clapton, from his coat pocket. "Can I play it?" he asked.

"By all means, Shawn, crank it up," I replied.

Devon slid his latest graffiti drawing from the storage rack and began to work. The screaming of B. B. and Eric's guitars filled the room and I began to think I might be passing their tests.

I started to work, painting one of the slats of the basket dark blue. Antoine gestured toward a carton of plaster-infused gauze and asked, "Think you could show me how to use that stuff to make my hand?"

"I'd be glad to, Antoine. Do you want to build an armature—like a skeleton—to place the plaster cloth on, or do you want to wrap it around your own hand?"

"My hand," he said.

"Okay, the first step is to cut the cloth into strips about 2 inches wide. Let me know when you get 25 strips cut." I handed Antoine a pair of scissors and started back toward my basket. Immediately there was an almost palpable tension in the studio. The other boys watched closely. Antoine cleared his throat and said, "Staff wouldn't like it if I use these. I'm only on Phase 2 [referring to the facility's 4-stage privilege and responsibility level system] I ain't allowed."

"I tell you what, Antoine. How about bringing the box of plaster cloth over to where I'm painting? If we're right beside each other it'll be almost like I am the one using the scissors."

I returned to my basket and Antoine brought over a large roll of plaster cloth and the scissors so that he could work beside me. When he'd cut all the strips he asked, "Now what?"

I pointed toward a cabinet along the wall and said, "You'll find a jar of Vaseline in one of those drawers. Slather one hand with it and then I will help you apply the plaster cloth."

When Antoine indicated that he was ready I said, "Now decide how you want to position your hand."

From the other side of the room Francisco piped up, "I bet I know what he'd like to do with that hand." The other boys chuckled.

I said, "Yes, well, I suppose there are times when we all are tempted to express ourselves that way. But in this group we are all about finding our own unique ways to express feelings. How do you want your hand positioned, Antoine?"

"Like a fist, man."

"That's fine," I said. "Make a fist, and keep your hand still. This is going to take a while." I proceeded to dip strips of plaster cloth in a bowl of warm water and wrap Antoine's clenched fist with several layers." His peers watched this procedure closely.

About 15 minutes later, with some alarm in his voice, Antoine said, "This is getting really hot."

I replied, "That is just a chemical reaction as the plaster dries. Nothing to worry about, Antoine."

"Feels weird, Dr. Bruce."

"Again, nothing to worry about, but make sure you keep your fingers still." Several minutes later I checked the progress of the drying plaster and found that it was firm enough to be removed. "All right, Antoine, I need you to hold still now while I cut this off."

As I approached him with the roundnose scissors he seemed wary. "You sure you know what you're doing?"

I adopted an accent and said, "Never fear, Dr. Bruce has performed this operation many times before." I made two cuts in the plaster on opposite sides of Antoine's wrist and eased the cast off of his hand. He then used additional plaster cloth strips to repair the slits.

As that session neared its end and we were cleaning up, Shawn retrieved his CD. I said, "Shawn, that was great. Thanks a lot for bringing B. B. and Clapton to our group." He smiled hesitantly.

Francisco lagged behind as the others were leaving the studio. "My little sister's birthday is in a couple weeks. I wanna make her a Mexican flag. You cool with that?"

"Do you want to draw it or paint it?"

"No, if you say okay, I wanna use some cloth and put it together with thread."

I was surprised. "You know how to sew?"

"Yeah, I can do that."

"That would be great, Francisco. You can get that going next week."

During the next several sessions, Francisco cut, pieced, and sewed together strips of red, white, and green cloth. Devon worked on increasingly elaborate graffiti drawings, Shawn brought music and kept the beat for the group, and I painted images of feelings on the slats of the baskets (Figures 2 & 3 & Plates 2 & 3).

Figure 2. Basket Detail #1

In the next session there were some interesting developments. First, Shawn brought a CD by Bob Dylan to play. I said, "Shawn, Bob is my favorite songwriter. How did you know?"

He half smiled and said, "I overheard you talking with one of the staff members once."

Second, when Shawn put Dylan in the player, he kept the volume fairly low. Third, he asked, "What's yer basket thing about?"

"It's about us."

Devon said, "Like we're all part of it . . . holdin' it together."

"Yes, Devon. Like that."

Antoine said, "You oughta have all our names on there someplace."

Figure 3. Basket Detail #2

I looked at him and replied, "That's a great idea. Maybe each of you could sign it."

Francisco said, "Nah, man, it's yours. You gotta do the signin'."

Shawn suggested that they all give me a sample of their signatures so that I could include them somewhere on the piece. Just then one of the attendants walked past the studio entrance. Devon called out to her, "Ms. D, Ms. D., come 'ere an' take look at this."

Ms. D. entered. Devon pointed to the basket and said, "That's about us. All of us, and Dr. Bruce."

Ms. D. said, "There is a lot going on in there."

"Yeah, and Dr. Bruce is gonna put our names on it someplace," Antoine said (see Figure 4 & Plate 4).

Figure 4. The Names

Over the next several months, Devon drew out his story in tag letters, and sometimes wild, sometimes funny, caricature portraits of people in his life. Antoine created intriguing bas-relief plaster sculptures of fists, open hands, and a wounded heart. Francisco sewed the Mexican flag for his little sister, another for his grandmother, and another for his primary therapist at the facility. Shawn wrote poetry, and I filled the basket with the feelings that, as Devon had said, "we were all holdin' together." Making art together over a period of 6 months reduced their isolation and created a sense of connection. Each of those young men found their own distinct way to express feelings and each had his own unique journey, yet paradoxically they all learned to travel together and, within the confines of the studio, they constructed a therapeutic community.

Chapter VI

HOW YOU FEEL ABOUT ME AND HOW
I FEEL ABOUT YOU

The process of creating objects–artworks–distinguishes the work of art-based therapy groups from other modes of group therapy. Art therapy group leaders have a distinct advantage over psychologists, social workers, psychiatrists, and counselors who must rely on verbal interactions in their group work. The painting, sculpture, or other art form is the focal object, and it is during the creative process that the relationships among group members and the group leader are constructed. Artworks and the creative process provide subjects and contexts for the group members to be together in relationship. Sometimes the artworks are spoken about, and sometimes members are asked to give their images a voice and speak from the perspective of their artworks.

The shared experience of creating art and dialoguing with images in a group setting offers rich opportunities to explore how members feel about themselves, one another, and the group leader. Making art can also help motivate members of therapy groups to explore aspects of their interpersonal relationships in safe, nonthreatening ways. Sometimes, a carefully considered common artistic task can gently cut through members' defenses that could otherwise disrupt a group's therapeutic work. An example of this function of group art making happened when I was leading a group class in a graduate art therapy program.

After meeting with the group of students for several sessions, I was frustrated by the superficial level of interaction. Members of the group seemed committed to keeping the tone light. The students gossiped and told funny stories, and subtly resisted all attempts on my part to help the group move to a deeper level of relating to one another.

After one such session, I talked about my experience of the group with a faculty colleague, and told her I was frustrated by the students' apparent desire to remain on the surface, and to keep their relationships superficial. "They keep reminding me that this is only a class, not real therapy, I complained. "Although it's true that it is a class and they are students, it bothers me that they seem to be resisting the opportunity to genuinely relate to one another."

My colleague responded, "It sounds like the group is just floating on the water, not really diving into the depths." Her comment stayed with me and I decided to use her metaphor of the ocean with my students.

At the beginning of the next art therapy class session, I taped a 12-foot-long piece of brown kraft paper to one of the studio walls. I then asked the students to select a piece of blue or green chalk and work together to cover the entire paper. "Don't let any of the brown paper show through," I instructed. As they worked to obliterate the brown paper, group members inevitably bumped into one another. Chalk dust flew, and an amiable hum of conversation and laughter arose that suggested they were enjoying this simple task.

When the paper was covered, I gave each member of the group a paper towel and asked them to blend the colors. The result was a mottled background of subtle shades of green and blue. Addressing the group, I said, "We have created an underwater world. What I want us to do now is draw ourselves into this ocean. Portray yourself as some element or character that represents how you see yourself in this group. For example, you might be a sea creature, rock, or some kind of plant."

A flurry of activity ensued. One of the women drew pieces of coral. Another portrayed a stingray, and yet another represented her involvement in the group by drawing tendrils of seaweed extending across the paper. A fourth student portrayed herself as the fish Nemo from the popular animated children's movie. I drew an open oyster with a large pearl within. Like before, there was chatter and social banter. One of the students was markedly quiet as she drew a caricature of a puffer fish.

After we completed our drawings, we arranged our chairs in a semicircle facing the forest mural as we discussed the images. Predictably, an air of surface humor marked the conversation, and members of the group avoided serious consideration of how the images might symbolize roles that they played. Comments were made about the beautiful coral, and the loveable Nemo. One student said that she'd had a salad made from kelp. When it came time for Mary, the woman who had drawn the puffer fish, to talk about her image, one of the group members said, "Oh, that puffer looks so cute."

Mary chuckled and countered, "Well, I may be cute, but you better watch out for those spines. They will hurt you if you get too close."

I said, "It looks like the fish is all puffed up."

She replied, "Yes, they do that when they are in danger."

Another group member smiled and commented, "It doesn't look too threatening to me." This comment elicited nods of agreement from other members of the group, and one student added, "I just loved *Finding Nemo*." This inspired several remarks about favorite movies.

I sat silent for several moments, waiting for the conversation to wind down. Finally, the group became aware of my stillness and turned toward me. Addressing the puffer fish image, I asked, "Puffer, your spines are bristling; are you feeling frightened in this ocean?" I turned toward the student artist.

An uncomfortable silence followed. Mary took a deep breath and said, "Yes, I am scared in this class."

Other members of the group rushed in to ease the tension, assuring Mary that there was nothing to be afraid of, and joking that no one would dare try to harm such a cute blowfish.

Without acknowledging the superficial reassurances of the group, I again turned my attention toward the image of the fish. "Puffer, do you know what scares you about this ocean?" I asked.

Mary thought for a moment and then replied, "People may not like this, but I think this ocean is a fake. It's all just an illusion."

The student who'd drawn the stingray jumped in, "Of course we are pretending. We can't really be sea creatures; this is just fun."

Mary turned toward her peer and replied, "That's the problem, isn't it? We are all just pretending all the time." Tears formed in her eyes as she continued, "Here we are in the program because we want to be art therapists, and we say we want to help people use art to heal, but we sit around and act like this is some kind of a party. You might not want to hear it, but yes, I am scared. I am scared that we are missing something and we don't even know how to be real with each other."

A few moments of uncomfortable silence followed. Then, referring to my drawing, I said, "I drew myself as the oyster with a pearl." No one responded. I went on, "Do you know how pearls are made?"

Again, no one replied. "Well, you see, oysters get a piece of sand caught in their soft inner tissue and it hurts them, I explained. "To ease the pain they cover the piece of sand with a creative juice that makes it easier to tolerate. But then that gets hard, too, and it hurts. So the oyster coats it again. This happens many times over until what is left is a pearl. The ugly hurtful piece of sand is transformed by the creative juice and made beautiful."

One of the students said, "That's a nice little story, Bruce. But what is your point?"

I was about to respond when Mary spoke. "I think he is saying that we need to get in touch with, and share, our pieces of sand with each other."

"You are right on, Mary. If we are going to really get to know one another, to see the beauty in one another, we have to look at the painful pieces of our lives. Genuine relationships—the kind of relationships you will want to have with your clients in the future—cannot be formed out of cuteness. Real relationships have to be deeper than that."

One of the students protested, "But this is just a class. This isn't a real therapy session."

Mary responded, "But if we don't risk being real with each other here, how will we be able to do it when we are out in our clinical settings?"

At that point I suggested that we take a good look at our drawings and think about how we might be relating like the stingray, the seaweed, Nemo, and the puffer fish. "I suspect there might even be some shark lurking in us all."

The group class was never quite the same after that session. The images from the ocean and Mary's frightened puffer prompted the group to decide to engage in authentic relationships.

In our culture, people often choose to relate to others in superficial ways. We see a friend in passing and ask, "How are you?" A typical response is, "Fine." We can be taken aback when someone responds with an honest expression of emotion.

The beauty of making art is that it reveals the truth of how we feel. My art therapy mentor, Don Jones, was fond of saying, "Nothing ever happens by accident in art." Whether we consciously intend to or not, creative activity allows us to get beneath the surface and helps us express what is really happening in our lives. Lines, shapes, colors, forms, and images provide a mirror that reflects the mysteries: the good, the bad, the ugliness, and the beauty that is within us all. The process of looking into such mirrors, in the company of others, creates a safe venue for expressing how you feel about me and how I feel about you.

In art-based group therapy, artworks are the primary mode of communication, and the creative process is the venue in which authentic relationships among group members and the group leader are formed. Artistic activity is both the subject and the context that facilitate group members being together in relationship.

The process of creating artworks affords group members and the group leader an objective thing to talk with and about. Clients often find that talking about the characters or artistic elements in their artworks is less threatening than directly discussing feelings and treatment issues. In the example above, Mary was able to give form to her fears of, and desire for, more meaningful relationships with her classmates.

Generally speaking, it is safe to assume that clients referred to art-based therapy groups have already tried to remedy their problems through individual verbal therapy or traditional talk-based group psychotherapy without significant relief. The reasons for the failure of verbal therapy groups are, of course, as numerous and varied as the clients themselves.

Ralph's Monolith

I met Ralph when he was referred to an art-based therapy group that I led at a psychiatric hospital. The treatment team hoped that the group would help Ralph express his feelings and enhance his interpersonal relating skills. He was an angry and rough-edged 35-year-old, who'd been admitted to the hospital upon the recommendation of his lawyer. Ralph was facing a contentious divorce, and his lawyer hoped that a mental health evaluation could benefit his cause.

Ralph was a big man, 6 feet tall and weighing 225 pounds. He was not happy about being in the hospital, and he was uncooperative, despite the fact that he had signed a voluntary admission agreement. Within the first few hours of hospitalization, he had established a pattern of intimidating other clients and members of the staff. He was loud and offensive.

He came to the art group on the third day of his hospitalization. He'd been in the group for only a few minutes when his verbal assault began. He raised his voice and said, "This is bizarre. Why do they want me play around with crayons?"

"Ralph," I responded, "I know that doing art is often something that people have not done for a long time when they come here. But in this group we think that it is a good thing to do, and it might help us get to know you better." I sensed that Ralph's bluster might be covering feelings of inadequacy and sadness. The volume level and tone of his hostility seemed to belay an edge of desperation.

He snarled, "So whaddaya want me to do?"

In that group we started with a ritual of sitting in a circle, where I would ask all of the members individually what they were bringing with them on that day. I introduced Ralph to the group, and then initiated the check-in. Steve said, "It's been a tough day." Arlene offered, "I'm looking forward to seeing my family this afternoon." Other members made similarly innocuous comments. Andy, who was the senior member of the group, said, "I feel like Sisyphus, just pushing the rock." When it was Ralph's turn he grumbled, "I don' know what you all are talking about. I got nothing to say."

Addressing the group, I said, "I am struck by what Andy said about Sisyphus. Sisyphus was a figure of Greek mythology who was condemned to repeat forever the same meaningless task of pushing a rock up a mountain, only to see it roll down again. Let's use that as our art task today. Imagine the rocks in your own life and try to draw the scene."

Everyone in the group moved to their individual workspaces and started to draw their responses to the assignment except Ralph. He remained seated, and said to me, "I don't get it. What do you want me to do?"

I approached him and elaborated, "Well, just think about something that is hard in your life. What kind of a rock are you pushing?"

"You want me to think about a rock? How's that gonna help me?" he asked.

"Well, everyone in this group is facing difficult times." I said. "And you seem to be a really strong guy. Maybe if you draw your rock, it will help us understand how you feel."

Ralph bristled, "I don't have any feelings! But if I did, I don't see that they are anyone else's business but mine."

From where he was working, Andy said, "Everybody's got feelings, man."

Ralph glared over at him. "Who asked you?"

I interjected, "Ralph, one thing we ask of everyone in the group is that we all respect what others say. I know a lot of people here have a long history of not being taken seriously, and I promise you that we will take your feelings seriously."

He stared at the floor and muttered, "I already said I don't have any feelings."

Arlene spoke up. "Bruce says that the only people who don't have any feelings are just numb, or dead."

Ralph looked up, and I asked, "Are you numb, or dead?"

He grimaced. "I ain't neither one."

"That's good to know, Ralph, because we don't work with dead people in this group." The other group members chuckled, and Ralph almost smiled at that. "So, what would your rock look like?"

He looked down again and thought for a moment, then offered, "It'd be a big one."

"Okay," I said. "I motioned toward a table and asked, "How about trying to draw it?"

"So how do I start?" he asked. "I don't know how to draw a rock."

I asked him what the weather would be like in the place where his rock was sitting and he replied, "Stormy."

I gathered a box of chalk pastels and suggested that he work on a large sheet of black construction paper. "Let's begin by covering the paper with clouds." Ralph looked perplexed. I suggested that he start by using black, white, and blue pastels in swirling motions. "Don't think about it too much, just cover the page."

When he had done so, I showed him how to use a paper towel in continuous long strokes to blend the chalk across the page. I could tell by the look on his face that he was gratified when the colors blended together as he swirled the paper towel.

"Hey, this is cool," he said.

When he'd finished blending, I asked Ralph to imagine the shape of his boulder.

He responded, "I don't know, just rock-shaped I guess."

"Well, you said it was big. Would it be round, or square, or rectangular?"

"Sort of like that rock in *Space Odyssey 2001*," he offered.

"Ah, great image," I said. "Try to draw it over your storm."
When he finished that task, I praised his effort.
"Now what?" he queried.

Figure 5. Ralph's Monolith

I asked him what color the rock should be.

"Just black."

When he filled the rock shape with black, he seemed pleased with the result. His drawing of the 2001 monolith surrounded by swirling blue-gray clouds was both stark and turbulent (see Figure 5 & Plate 5).

When all of the members of the group had completed their drawings we reconvened in the circle of chairs and placed our images before us. Andy's drawing depicted an irregularly shaped fieldstone. Arlene's was a smooth, circular disk. Steve had drawn a pile of rocks. My drawing was of a piece of coal with a diamond emerging from it (see Figure 6 & Plate 6).

Figure 6. Coal and Diamond

Addressing the group, I said, "Rather than talk about these rocks, let's imagine we were going to hang them in a gallery. How would we arrange them?"

After some consideration, Steve remarked, "This reminds me of Stonehenge."

Andy commented, "Stonehenge—that's like a sacred place or something, right?"

Hesitantly, Arlene said, "Ralph's is the biggest. Maybe his should go in the middle."

I suggested, "Let's try moving them around. Ralph, is it okay with you if we put your drawing in the middle of the circle?"

Ralph seemed vaguely pleased, and yet uneasy, at the notion that his work would be the center of attention. Sheepishly, he said, "Yeah, that's okay."

Andy placed Ralph's drawing in the middle of the floor. For the next several minutes, the members of the group placed and re-placed their drawings in various configurations around Ralph's monolith. Without saying so out loud, each member symbolically experimented with where he or she felt most comfortable in relation to Ralph. Simultaneously, he grappled with their unspoken efforts to place themselves in relation to his drawing.

I do not think that this kind of relationship work could have been done in a group setting that relied upon words. In a verbal psychotherapy group, Ralph would likely have used his words to belittle and intimidate others and to keep his distance. The monolith drawing was a safe way for Ralph to symbolize his feelings of turmoil and loneliness, and to let those feelings be seen by his peers. In turn, group members were able to see beyond Ralph's hostile veneer, and through our images—a pile of rocks, an obelisk, a fieldstone, and lump of coal— we were able to begin the process of forming relationships with him.

Ralph's experience in the art-based therapy group offered hints that there was more to him than the angry and uncouth façade he initially displayed. In subsequent sessions, images of his fears, regrets, and inadequacies emerged. He talked very little about his artworks, but they spoke for him eloquently. In rare moments, Ralph was able to use words to amplify his images. But whenever it was directly suggested that the feelings he associated with his pictures might be his own, he quickly retreated into his defensive style of interaction. As long as his art piece was the subject of conversation, he would stick with it, but as soon as Ralph himself became the focus, his machismo would return. Through his images, he was able to share feelings of emptiness, anger, and sadness. These aspects of self may never have been known had it not been for his involvement in the art group.

Chapter VII

ART MAKING IN THE PRESENT TENSE

Making art is a sensual experience. Oil painters smell turpentine and feel the roughness of the canvas as brushes or palette knives scumble across the surface. Ceramicists' hands feel the slippery ooze of wet clay spinning on the wheel. Deep in their muscles and bones sculptors feel the pounding of hammers against chisels, chisels against stones. Dancers feel the weight of their bodies on the floor. Guitarists feel the vibrations of strings in their fingertips. Singers feel the vibrations of their vocal chords, and the movement of air from their lungs. Eyes strain, muscles cramp, and sweat runs. The arts bring pleasure and promote a sensual relationship with materials and images. Art processes demand that artists touch the world. Yet there is also a playful and mysterious quality to art that brings imagination into our daily lives. The arts evoke and intensify feelings; they provide a safe structure for expression in the present tense.

In the literature of verbal group psychotherapy, the principle of working in the here and now is a venerated principle. Yalom (2005), Rutan et al. (2007), Corey et al. (2008), and many other writers have devoted much energy to describing the complexity and importance of encouraging psychotherapy group members to stay in the here and now. In fact, Yalom went so far as to suggest that the here-and-now principle is perhaps the most important. He described a two-tiered process in which group members first *experience* the group and develop strong feelings toward one another and the group leader and, second, *illuminate* or examine and come to understand the group process.

One of the advantages that art-based therapy groups have over other forms of group therapy is the sensuality of art making. When an artist's body is involved in creating it is nearly impossible to not be in the present moment. Even when a client in a group is creating an artwork that specifically depicts an event from his or her past, the process of making is in the present. Janson (1971) offered the metaphor of a web of art comprised of all the strands of artistic tradition: Each new artwork emerges from those that came before. Thus, as group members make art, they add strands to the web of tradition, thereby connecting themselves with all that has already occurred in the history of art–and all that will be in the future–as they create in the present.

Sonia's Moves

When Sonia entered the art therapy group room she moved heavily, as if she were carrying a tremendous burden. I introduced her to the other adult group members and explained, "This is a group in which we make art as a way of getting in touch with and sharing feelings." I asked if she had ever tried to express her feelings artistically.

"No," Sonia replied, "I haven't done artwork since I left middle school."

"Well, that's fine, this'll be something new and different for you," I told her.

Sonia retorted, "This sounds juvenile to me."

"I suppose some people might think that," I said. "But I think art is a good way to express your feelings, and it can be a fun too."

Sonia seemed skeptical. "What are we supposed to do?" she asked.

"In a moment, we'll come up with a group theme to work from, and then we'll make art for awhile," I explained. "When we're done, we'll spend some time talking about the pictures. At the end of the session you can do whatever you'd like to do with your artwork, keep it or throw it away."

Sonia frowned and asked, "What's the point of making something if you are just going to throw it away?"

"You can keep your work if you want to, Sonia, but that's not the point," I said.

Another group member said, "You'll get used to it. It is a little embarrassing at first, but Bruce always says 'trust the process,' and it can really feel good sometimes."

Addressing the group, I announced, "Today, as a way of getting warmed up, I'd like you to close your eyes and move." I demonstrated. "Try to stay in one place so you don't bump into things. Okay, let's move." After a couple of minutes had passed, I said, "Okay, you can stop and open your eyes. Now, using whatever materials you want, try to recreate your movement in an art piece. Again, just let your body move."

There were some mild protestations, but eventually everyone was doing what I'd asked them to do. The room filled with the subtle sounds and rhythms of chalk on paper, paint on canvas, paper being torn and used in collage, and clothing rustling. We worked for an hour or so on our art pieces, and then I asked the members of the group to look around at their peers' work.

Sonia had used a thick brush to apply several layers of tempera paint to a large sheet of off-white tagboard. Her initial layer of paint was dark blue, mottled with black. Over that she had added gentle, swirling strokes of robin's egg blue and white. Despite the dark undercoat, the painting had a whimsical and open feel.

I commented, "I watched you paint for a moment, and now your piece makes me think of Ginger Rogers and Fred Astaire."

Sonia laughed. "When I was little, my friends and I used to love those old Hollywood musicals. We'd make stages out of pieces of plywood and put on shows for the whole neighborhood."

Aimee, one of the other group members, said, "Your painting looks like it has light and dark motions."

"I haven't thought about those old neighborhood plays for a long time," Sonia reflected.

Larry, another member, said, "I used to put on magic shows when I was a kid." He demonstrated the old stealing-your-nose thumb trick. Everyone in the group laughed.

I refocused on Sonia's painting. "Sounds like a good memory." I said.

She replied, "Yes, it is a good memory, but it makes me feel sad thinking about it."

Aimee asked, "What's the sadness about?"

Sonia breathed heavily and averted her eyes. "I don't know . . . it's been a long time since I felt like I was able to dance. These days I don't feel good about anything."

"Our artworks don't lie," I remarked. "If the light and whimsy were not a part of you, you would not have painted them. Your painting is very powerful, Sonia."

"I think I'll keep it," she said.

There is tremendous therapeutic value inherent in the process of making art in a group setting. Fleeting moments of perception, elusive bits of light and shadow, movements, sounds, and physical sensations are captured as group members create and respond to one another.

As Sonia's participation in the group unfolded, it was intriguing to watch her reclaim her life force. In the art therapy group room she rediscovered her capacity to move lightly and to relish the company of others. Her creative process reconnected her with her own dynamic internal energy, and she experimented with her imagination in the present. Even though many of her artworks dealt with issues from the past, the creative process and the finished works were potent expressions in the present tense.

Chapter VIII

THE EMPOWERING QUALITY OF MAKING
ART WITH OTHERS

The persons who come to art-based therapy groups often feel as though they have little or no power to effect change in their lives. Their sense of personal power has been wounded. They often feel victimized by circumstances and relationships. It is critical that art therapy group leaders work with clients to restore their awareness and faith in their own power.

Empowerment is not a phenomenon that can be accomplished through a combination of experiences and verbalization. Creative self-expression in the presence of others fosters group members' abilities to reclaim power and the accompanying responsibilities that come with power. Art-based group leaders are in an ideal position to facilitate the process of empowerment in clients by virtue of our own experiences with art making. In group contexts, art brings meaning to life by transforming conflict and ennobling painful struggle. An important task for art group leaders is to inspire group members to use their discomforts rather than be abused by them. Creative empowerment provides members with a process of transformation from the position of victims to that of survivors.

As human beings we are comprised of opposing forces, inconsistencies, and contradictions. We are in a state of continual change. Conflict and struggle are inevitable in our lives. This reality often engenders a core tension within that is expressed through our polarities. Art does not lessen this tension, but rather accentuates it by using the energy in empowering creative actions. The members of art-based groups can create meaning in their lives as they shape and color the distressing disharmony within themselves. Creative activity does not banish pain or discomfort: rather, it honors experiences that are diffi-

cult. Through the creative process of art making, contradictions and
conflicts are brought into focus. The empowering nature of artistic self-
expression does not seek to cure; instead, it accepts and ennobles the
struggles of life. Art brings our fears, loneliness, and anguish close to
us. It does not rid us of difficulties, but it enables us to live courageously in their presence. This is especially true of art that is made in
the presence of others.

As group members work together, they have the ultimate power to
change their creations. They can add color, darken, or highlight.
Indeed, artists can paint over the piece and start again. In this, artistic
activity is a metaphor for life itself. We can make mistakes, back up,
and try again. Artworks and life can be changed if and when people
decide to change. Initially, group members may not believe that they
have such power over the course of their lives, and for them, art making becomes an introduction into free will and the power of choice and
creation. To empower means to give authority to, or legal power to, or
to enable. Making art with others empowers.

Karen: "Things Remembered, Things Reversed"

Karen had heard about the outpatient art therapy group I was leading from a friend. She told me during our pre-group meeting that she
felt uneasy about seeking therapy of any kind. When I asked her to
explain, she said that she wasn't sure her problems really warranted
professional help. "I'm probably just feeling sorry for myself," she
said. Later in our conversation she told me that she wanted to try out
the group, but she wasn't willing to commit to therapy just yet. I
assured her that she would be free to discontinue participation in the
group if she didn't find it helpful, but that it would work best if she
gave it at least a few sessions before she made up her mind.

When Karen arrived at the appointed time, I was struck by my first
impressions of her. She was a middle-aged woman, slightly built, and
she moved in an apprehensive and burdened manner. As she introduced herself to the other members of the group, she established eye
contact awkwardly.

As the group members sat in a circle of chairs, Karen shared that her
father had died recently and that this had stirred up unresolved feelings of anger toward him. She said that he had been a distant yet dom-

ineering figure in her life that she had repeatedly rebelled against. "I spent so much time resisting him, and now . . . I miss him." There was palpable sadness in her eyes.

Tanya, a college student, replied, "That sounds familiar."

Karen added, "But I'm still not sure that I should be here."

Eric, another group member, chimed in, "That sounds familiar too."

"Everyone in this group has their own reasons for being here," I said. "I think almost everybody started out with a lot of questions. But the whole point of being in the group is to find ways to express feelings artistically, and to share those feelings with others."

Jen, a woman about the same age as Karen, urged, "Don't worry about not knowing why you're here. Give it some time and the answers will come."

I said, "Well, let's get started. Eric, what do you want to work on today?"

"I want to keep working on my painting," Eric replied.

"Jen, how about you?"

Jen said, "I've been thinking about what you said last session about feelings being neither good or bad. That has stuck with me. I think I will do a collage about that."

Tanya indicted that she wanted to work with clay.

When it was Karen's turn to focus her work she said, "I'm not much of an artist, but I like to put things together–just different things."

I replied, "Like found object art."

"I guess that's what they call it," Karen said.

"Okay, let's work for an hour or so, then we will reconvene." As the other group members gathered their materials, I took Karen on a quick tour of the studio and showed her where things were kept.

Karen decided to use a wooden cigar box as the starting point for her art piece, but she said, "I'm not sure where to begin."

I smiled. "I probably have some suggestions about how to start, but you have to help me."

"How could I help you?" she asked.

I replied, "You probably don't want the 'White Owl' sign to show, so how about starting with painting the box."

"What color should I use?"

"It will probably take more than one coat, so start by using gesso to get a base coat." I gestured toward the paint cabinet. "You'll find the gesso in there."

This was how Karen entered the art-based group. She was struggling with feelings of loss and loneliness and unfinished anger, but still seemed interested in life. She did not seem resentful about her situation, just weighed down. By the end of that first session, I was convinced that the group could be of help to Karen, and I was certain that engaging in art processes would benefit her.

In subsequent sessions she told stories about her father. She painted each surface of the box and then added an assortment of small stones and other objects to the interior. She did not say much about what these items represented.

She brought a selection of family photographs to the fourth or fifth session. As the other members of the group worked on their various pieces, Karen sat at a table by herself, looking through the pictures. One of the photos was of her and her father sitting at a picnic table facing away from one another. I watched as she tentatively placed it in one position after another on the inside of the box. Each time she would place the photo, sit back and consider it, and then move it to a different location.

When the group reconvened in the circle I asked, "Karen, would you like to start our discussion today?"

She nodded affirmatively, but said nothing.

After a moment, I said, "I noticed that you couldn't seem to decide what you wanted to do."

She picked up the photo of her and her father. "I got stuck today. I brought this picture and wanted to put it somewhere, but then it didn't seem right."

Eric asked, "Can we see the picture?"

She handed the photograph to him. Eric looked, then passed it on to the others.

When Tonya held the photo she said, "You guys don't look too happy here."

Karen closed her eyes for a moment, then opened them and said, "That was taken on my seventeenth birthday. I don't know why, but leading up to that day I got the feeling that my parents were going to give me a car. We had a party in our backyard and when I opened my presents . . . there was no car."

Jen said, "That must have been disappointing."

Tears formed in Karen's eyes. "It was stupid, I guess. I mean, a car is a pretty big thing. My dad asked me what was the matter and I just blurted out that I thought they were giving me a car. My dad laughed at me and said that I'd have to earn a car." Tears slid from Karen's eyes.

Eric asked, "How did you respond to him?"

Karen stared at the floor and sighed. "I said something awful. I don't remember what exactly, but I know it was hurtful and mean."

The group was silent for a minute.

Karen went on, "It was always like that with him. Nothing was ever just given, everything had to be earned, and it seemed like whatever I did I was never good enough!"

Jen started to respond, but Karen interrupted. "But that still doesn't excuse what I said. Now that he's gone, I can't tell you how many times I have wished that I could take back what I said. But I never did."

The picture had made its way around the circle and I held it. "This photo must have been taken after—"

Karen retrieved it from my hand. "Yes. It just about sums up our relationship."

"I wonder," I pondered. "If you could change the picture, how would it be different?"

Karen placed the photo on the floor. "It can't be changed. It is what it is."

I responded, "You can't undo what happened, Karen, but for the sake of your art piece you could rework it."

"I don't know how," she said.

Tanya suggested, "You could scan it into the computer and then reverse the image in Photoshop."

"I'm not very tech savvy," Karen replied.

"I'm good with Photoshop. I will help you," Tanya offered.

Karen and Tanya agreed to work together during the next session to scan, copy, and reverse the image.

In the next session, when their manipulation of the photograph was complete, Karen had a new image of her and her father facing one another. She fastened that image to the inside of the painted cigar box lid. As her final act, she glued glitter letters to the outside of the lid: "Things Remembered, Things Reversed."

Karen completed a number of other projects while in the art group. Small, intricate sculptures comprised of miscellaneous objects from her life and the studio. Through making things, and sharing them with her peers in the group, Karen ennobled her struggle with letting go of her hard feelings toward her father and her own harsh self-judgments. She transformed her anger and pain into artworks. This did not make the pain and anger go away, but it helped her accept these feelings, and it eased her burden. Karen stopped being controlled by her feelings of anger and regret and was able to use those feelings as the source of her creative work. This enabled her to live courageously in the presence of her feelings of anger, sadness, and remorse. The found object sculptures provided an artistic chronicle of her therapeutic work. She moved from the position of someone burdened by words she could not take back to that of a woman accepting, and even celebrating, memories of her father. As she discovered the artistic power of reworking and changing direction with her images, Karen embraced her power over her own existence.

Making art with others fosters a sense of personal and communal empowerment.

Chapter IX

REGARD FOR OTHERS

In art-based therapy, it is helpful for group leaders to explore ways of being with artworks and the artists who create them that honor the complexities of their existence. McNiff (1992) wrote, "Symbols and art works exist to express the unexplainable, and they continuously generate different responses within the same person" (p. 97). When members of a group create art they are making visible pieces of their own story, shards of multifaceted and unexplainable realities. Artists reveal themselves to others in the group through their creative processes, artistic representations, and verbal narratives and dialogues. Although no single artwork is a complete portrait of the artist, every image a group member creates is a partial self-portrait that metaphorically represents that artist's life.

Art group leaders model a regard for members' artworks that is based upon compassionate and sustained observation of the physical qualities of the work. Careful, empathic consideration conveys a sense of respect for the autonomy of the artwork that in turn metaphorically conveys respect for the artist who created the work. Although artworks are often mysterious and perplexing, they always hold multiple truths that are open to many valid interpretations. In my groups, I approach clients' artworks with a sense of awe and wonder, and try to establish with each client a respectful conversation that embraces many possible meanings. In art-based group sessions, I engage in dialogue with clients and their artworks in an effort to invite both to share stories. Frequently, clients' art pieces are puzzling, disturbing, and hard to grasp. Still, in nearly every circumstance, when I can sustain attention and keep an open mind, images inevitably reveal meanings that are important to their creator.

According to Buber (1970), we frequently view objects through the lens of their functions. Unfortunately, we often regard people in the same way. Rather than making ourselves truly available to others, understanding them, and genuinely sharing with them, we distance ourselves and often remain apart from moments of potential relationship. We do this in order to protect our vulnerabilities or to attempt to get something from others. Buber calls such interactions *I-It.*

In contrast to *I-It* relationships, it is possible to put oneself completely into a relationship, to really be present with and understand another person, without masks and pretenses, even without words. Such moments of relating Buber called *I-Thou.* The relationship bonds that are created in *I-Thou* relationships enhance each participant, and each person responds by trying to improve the other person. The result is genuine, reciprocal, and authentic sharing.

Buber considered art, music, and poetry to be media that could stimulate and facilitate authentic relating. In art-based groups, I want to cultivate a sense of reverence for the "Other." Clients often come to art-based groups entrenched in *I-It* patterns of relating. Therapeutic techniques that attempt to intervene too directly in these patterns frequently fail because clients become frightened, defensive, and resistive. By subtly modeling *I-Thou* regard for artworks, art therapists can gently help clients make significant shifts in their relating styles in ways that ease clients' fears and circumvent defensive reactions.

I have often encountered adolescent and adult clients who declare that they do not care what others think of them. "As one 15-year-old girl said in reference to her peers in the art therapy group, 'They don't mean shit to me'" (B. Moon, 1998, p. 181). In my experience, however, if a client attends at least two or three group sessions, a very different persona may emerge. The quickest and most efficient way to form a solid therapeutic alliance with such clients is through making art rather than through discussion. By making, the artist takes images from within, works with them, and shares them with others who are in the group. This is an act of acknowledgment of the others beyond the boundaries of the self.

Individual meaning can be found only in the context of relationships with others, hence the importance of art therapy group work. The self that relates to others as *Its* must be transcended for personal meaning to be present. Through the creative process of making art, group members offer their views of their peers and their unique responses to the others in the group. In the context of relationship to the group, the individual member expresses his or her particular self. The others in the group give witness to the unique qualities of the individual artist and often create art in response. A circular process emerges as the group creates, the individual responds, the artist makes again, and the group attends.

Several years ago I taught a group dynamics course to first-year graduate students. The course was structured so that the first 90 minutes of each class session involved students in art-based group processes. In a sense, the students were able to simulate a therapy group, using the class as a laboratory in which they could experiment with interpersonal relating styles, leadership strategies, and art techniques. The last hour of each class session was devoted to discussing the preceding 90-minute group process in relation to the assigned readings for that day.

As the semester progressed there seemed to be a subtle, underlying edge of hostility and sarcasm that pervaded the members' interactions with one another. In post-group discussions, whenever I talked about my sense that there were feelings that were not being addressed by the group, the students either retreated into denial or used humor as a way to deflect and redirect the conversation. I was concerned because they seemed to be actively resisting forming genuine relationships with one another. This came to a head roughly halfway through the semester.

Brianna, a student who'd relocated from out of state to attend the graduate art therapy program, had been feeling homesick and depressed. During the art-making segment of the class she created a canvas bag that was reminiscent of the makeshift hobo's sacks one sees in photographs from the 1930s and '40s. As she talked about her art piece, which contained a number of objects that she said represented important aspects of her life, Brianna revealed that she was considering quitting the program and returning home. Another member of the class, Carolyn, had used modeling clay to sculpt a small female figure. She said that she was struggling with the question of how to inform her parents that she was pregnant. Other students were wrestling with feelings related to the stress of being in graduate school: anxiety, perfectionism, and fear of failure.

One member of the class, Lauren, had always participated in the art-making component of the class, but usually had little to say in response to her peers' artworks, and she seldom initiated interactions during the post-group discussions. On this occasion, however, Lauren's drawing was striking. She had used oil sticks on a large sheet of black tagboard to portray a vividly colored landscape. A black horse was rearing up on its hind legs, pawing at a bright sun in a vibrant sky, and there were ominous looking mountains in the distance. Lauren had worked quietly and because of the dramatic nature of Brianna's and Carolyn's expressions, her image had not drawn much attention. When her turn came to talk about her drawing with the group she said quietly, "I'm not sure what to say about this to you guys. It just is what it is."

"You don't have to say anything, Lauren," I said, "but wow, what a powerful piece!"

She looked at her drawing and sarcastically responded, "Yes, I know I don't have to talk about it."

Without reacting to her sarcasm I continued, "The most important thing is that you made art. Talking is fine, but it's not the main thing." I asked, "Are you interested in what others think about your work?"

She hesitated. "I suppose so, but really it's just a picture of a horse."

I then asked the group members if they had any reactions to Lauren's drawing.

Carolyn said, "When I look at your drawing, Lauren, the thing that really hits me is the wild look of that horse. It reminds me of the *Black Stallion* books I read when I was a kid."

Brianna said, "There is something sort of scary about the mountains. They look dark. I don't think I'd want to go there."

Shana, another student, added, "I love horses. He looks like he's free and just daring anyone to try and rope him, or even get too close."

As Lauren listened to these responses to her drawing she became sullen and seemed to withdraw. I asked, "Are these reactions to your work hard for you to hear?"

She said, "I don't know. Something about what Shana just said. . . ." She paused. "I don't feel very free. In fact, I feel anything but free." Tears formed in Lauren's eyes.

I commented, "It looks like you are experiencing some strong emotions."

Lauren grimaced, "If you must know, I don't like being here. I like the program okay, but I hate the cold. But I can't just pack up and go home." She turned toward Brianna with an almost accusatory glare.

Brianna said, "I had no idea you felt like I do."

Lauren reacted, "I am not quitter!" There was an almost tangible tension in the air.

I said, "Lauren, I wonder if you would be willing to work with your image?"

She paused, "It really is just a picture, but I guess so. What do you want me to do?"

"Would you mind standing up and trying to get into the pose that the horse is in?"

Lauren stood and reached out with her arms, one higher than the other, as if she was the horse pawing at the air. I asked, "Horse, when you look around yourself, what do you see?"

She thought for a moment. "Just wide open spaces. No one else is around."

I then asked, "Can you move like the horse in your picture?"

Lauren began to paw at the air in a hesitant and tentative manner. She seemed embarrassed and quickly lowered her arms. "Try to stick with it," I said.

"I feel foolish," she replied, and sat down.

We sat in silence for a minute or two. I said, "Hmm, the horse in your picture looks so wild."

"Like I said, it's just a picture."

I addressed the group as a whole, "Can anyone else imagine being that horse?"

Brianna spoke up, "I can."

"Okay, give it a try," I said.

Brianna stood and assumed a position similar to Lauren's. She closed her eyes and began to paw the air. At first she too was hesitant, but gradually her movements became more forceful and aggressive. After a minute or so she dropped her hands to her sides and breathed deeply, a light sheen of sweat on her face.

I asked, "Brianna, what are you feeling?"

Tears had formed in her eyes. She said, "I am so angry and lonely. It's almost like I want to hit something or someone, but there is nothing and no one to hit."

Lauren too had tears trickling down her cheeks. I asked if she wanted to say anything in response to Brianna's movement. She shook her head no, but she stood, walked across the room and extended her hand to Brianna. They shook hands and then gave one another a consoling hug. That session marked the beginning of a friendship between

Brianna and Lauren that continued throughout their two years in the graduate program, and it also marked the beginning of the entire group's entry into authentic relating.

The image of Lauren's horse and Brianna's response to it facilitated a bond that had important meaning for each of them. The other members of the class witnessed the creation of a genuine relationship and this became a meaningful event in the life of the group. They allowed themselves to move beyond defensive sarcasm and began to relate with one another in ways that transcended *I-It*. Through the creative process of making and responding artistically, group members were able to form authentic relationships with the others in the group.

In the art-based groups that I have led in psychiatric hospitals, residential treatment programs, and graduate art therapy training programs, we work with simple materials and artistic responsive techniques. With appropriate support and encouragement, nearly every group member ultimately experiences the positive influence of the creative energy of the group studio environment. Immersion in artistic processes creates a milieu that fosters positive regard among the members of the group. I recently received an e-mail from a former client, who after 20 years still carries the affirmative energy of art-based group work:

> I've never forgotten being in the art group down in the basement. We were all so angry and hurt, but somehow we were able to be different in the art room. Over the years, art has been a great companion. Pencil sketches on notebook paper, chalk on grocery bags, acrylic paint on canvas or whatever I could find to paint on—from coffee tables, to freezer paper. . . . It was a relief and a joy. Thanks for the little things that stick around for years.

Chapter X

MAKING ART WITH OTHERS IS GRATIFYING AND PLEASURABLE

The healing powers of art are infinitely adaptable. They can flow through any life situation and lend their transformative powers to people in need regardless of particular circumstances. The primary healing attribute of art involves the cultivation and release of creative energy and imagination (McNiff, 2003, 2009). This activation of creative energy can—and sometimes must—be done in the solitude of an artist's studio, or in the private confines of individual therapy. In my experience, however, group participation in art making can help individuals in ways that transcend solo activity.

For art therapists working with people who are suffering it is important to remember that it feels good to make art. Many clients initially enter art therapy groups with an attitude of distrust. They do not believe that making art in the company of others will help them; their problems are too complicated or serious to be eased by what they regard as a frivolous activity. Surely lurking within all clients, along with their wounds, there are joys as genuine and deep as their sorrows.

The simple act of making art in the presence of other people who are engaged in creative work can be deeply satisfying and gratifying. Artistic activity is a bridge between inner and outer realities and it is often cathartic, organizing, and integrative. Making art in the presence of others can evoke and intensify feelings while at the same time providing safe, concrete structures for their expression.

Even though client members of art-based therapy groups are intensely aware of the struggle, work, and pain their artworks reveal, it is the pleasure of the activity itself that enables the artist to face the burdens of self-expression. The pleasure of creative self-expression is heightened by the experience of group participation. In a sense, this is an altruistic example of herd behavior: individuals in a group acting together without planned direction in ways that are beneficial to all. McNiff (2003) used the metaphor of a slipstream to illustrate this point: "The practice of imagination orchestrates a community of creation that moves inside and outside the individual person" (p. 75).

Group participation in art making promotes sensual interactions with the environment. Oil paints, turpentine, markers, chalk, paper, and clay all have physical qualities, textures, and odors that permeate the studio. Creative activity encourages artists to touch the world and sensual experiences heighten self-awareness in ways that are pleasurable and gratifying.

The Opening Colloquium

A prime example of the positive energy generated by a community of creators is the annual opening colloquium experience in the graduate art therapy program at Mount Mary College. For twenty-five years Shaun McNiff served as the facilitator for the colloquium and his approach to working with large groups has shaped the design of the event. Early in the fall semester, approximately fifty students and members of the faculty participate in a weekend of immersion in art making and responsive processes in a lodge setting in the hills of southern Wisconsin. The opening colloquium sets the tone for the academic year and begins the work of developing the graduate art therapy community.

Typically, first-year students come to the colloquium with a measure of anxiety and self-doubt. Surrounded by relative strangers in a setting that is quite different from their normal college environment, they are unsure of what to expect from the weekend. Art therapy students frequently begin graduate school with the ingrained belief that their art process is a singular one best practiced in the solitude of their individual studio. Often they have had painful experiences with group critiques in undergraduate art courses that left them feeling defensive and devalued. In order to counteract participants' initial resistance to collective art making the faculty promotes a playful atmosphere as we begin to work together. Shaun always encourages us to use our bodies to make rhythms and sounds by clapping and foot stomping in unison as a way of freeing the imagination. Collective movement and expression is the primary vehicle for going beyond resistance. The group activity serves as a creative force that propels the individual person in ways that are not possible when working alone. The effect of people moving and making sounds together establishes a tangible flow that embraces and holds the individual.

Shaun's objective in this warm-up experience is rhythmic repetition. As students involve themselves in moving and making sounds, they gradually let go of inhibitions and become part of a larger movement and sound experience that stirs a sensibility to expressions that transcend what an individual is capable of doing single-handedly. The structure of the movement and sounds, coupled with the repetition of the expressions, makes the process accessible to the participants. When a student initially resists and does not join in, the rhythms and sounds continue and it is relatively difficult to remain aloof from the collective expression.

For new students this is often initially an experience that is outside their frame of reference and may push them beyond their comfort zones. In fact one of the underlying purposes of the opening colloquium is to help students begin to get comfortable with being uncomfortable. There are many times in the careers of art therapists when they are confronted with circumstances in relation to clients' expressions that are quite unnerving and so it is essential to develop the ability to remain present and engaged even when uncomfortable. Anyone who has participated in this sort of unrehearsed expressive experience knows that the rhythm of people moving and making sounds together will, as Shaun says, "take them to places they cannot go alone." As community members immerse themselves in the flow of kinetic and aural expression, it holds them and becomes the starting point for other visual and performance art forms.

Following the movement and sound warm-up experiences, Shaun helps the group expand the process of expression by engaging with the visual media chosen by each individual in response to the simple instruction to "make art from movement." The intent is to encourage students to turn off their analytic minds in relation to art making and let art emerge from the physical experience of movement (McNiff, 2003, 2009).

I recall one student, Ellen, who experienced some difficulty getting started painting in response to the "make art from movement directive." Shaun commented, "You look like you are stuck."

Ellen responded, "I don't know what you want me to do. This is not how I paint."

He asked, "How do you usually get started?"

"I have a mental image, something I am thinking about, and then I transfer that onto my canvas."

Shaun replied, "That is all well and good, and I am not suggesting that there is anything wrong with that kind of work. But for this weekend I'd like you to just try something different. Imagine painting from your thighs, your feet, and your lower body, and try and relax your mental controls and expectations."

Ellen said, "But I am afraid that I won't have any control and that the painting won't have a message."

"That's precisely the point," Shaun replied. "I am convinced that painting, all the arts really, are about movement. Every drawing, every painting is intimately connected with movement. In my own work I often have an idea or a central image, but I find that it is helpful to let go of that when I am painting and to let the movement take me where the piece needs to go."

Ellen said, "But all through art school I had to constantly defend my ideas, the genesis of my work."

Shaun responded, "I respect that, I really do. But in my role as the leader of this weekend I want to help the group realize that all you have to do is start moving and then stay with your gestures in order to allow them to unfold. The quality of movement expression is impeded when you think too much about preconceived images and put all your emphasis on planning. I am afraid that you will miss the opportunity to simply immerse yourself in the process of moving in the present moment. I urge you to concentrate on the movements you were doing earlier and not to worry about what will happen next. I tell people all the time, 'If you can move you can paint.' Just think of your painting as a record of your movement."

Although Ellen still appeared skeptical, she closed her eyes and reenacted the movements she had generated during the warm-up exercise. Then, with an oil stick in each hand, she recreated and spontaneously built upon those same gestures on her canvas. Over the next hour she covered the canvas with multiple layers of her bold gestures. The resulting artwork was vibrant, expressive, and filled with energy.

The many art forms that emerge from this work establish a creative environment that has more of an impact on participants than any preconceived image or predetermined therapeutic method could provide and it is, as Shaun says, accessible to people in every life situation. The process of making art together establishes a creative milieu that stimulates positive energy and shapes a therapeutic community of artists, artworks, and expressions that make up the core essence of art-based group therapy. The sum of these artistic processes constitutes the restorative energy of the environment that acts upon the participants.

After each individual has made an art piece, rather than engage in linear discussions or explanations of the participants' artwork, we encourage artistic responses to each person's creations. These responses may entail writing poetry, vocalization, movement, performance, drawing, painting, or sculpting. Regardless of the form, the intent is to respond to artworks through creative expression in lieu of verbal explanation. In this way we steer clear of assigning particular meanings to an artwork and more authentically react to the creative energy of the expression.

When the entire group gathered, Shaun asked if he could work with my painting in order to demonstrate this kind of responding (see Figure 7 and Plate 7).

I was prepared to talk about my associations to the path, pool of water, and turbulent sky. But rather than ask me questions about the meaning of my images, Shaun placed the painting on the floor in the middle of the circle of students.

Addressing the group he said, "My way of interacting with art objects and images is to respond to visual artworks with movements, vocalizations, performances, rituals, poems, imaginal dialogue, and other forms of creative expression. These actions invariably spiral into other forms of art." He looked intently at my painting. I recall feeling both mildly embarrassed and simultaneously honored by his concentrated attention. He then began to move. Initially his movements were small, repetitive circular gestures, mimicking the circular shapes of the moon and sky. Gradually his movements became more expansive, utilizing his entire body in stretching emulation of the gestures of my painting. As his movements evolved into more vigorous actions he emitted guttural sounds of exhalation that mirrored the exertion of his response.

His concentration on the painting and repetition of movement fostered a ritual-like performance atmosphere that saturated the lodge with a sense of sacredness. I was mesmerized, not only by the dance

Figure 7. Untitled Painting from Opening Colloquium

that Shaun created, but also by my sense that I was being held and responded to in a way that was clearly beyond words. After a couple minutes of watching his interaction with my painting I was speechless and immersed in a feeling of deep connection that defied narrative explanation. It was as if I was being known in a way that was nearly unfathomable. I remember having tears in my eyes when he finished. Even now as I write this, nearly two years after the fact, I am still struck by an ineffable feeling of reverence as I attempt to recount the event, and I know, although I struggle to explain why, that Shaun understood my expression. He got it. My experience of witnessing his response was profoundly healing, although I cannot say exactly what personal wound was being healed. I am still not precisely sure what the painting means, but I know that it has potent meanings for me, and that it feels good.

Having now participated in a good number of opening colloquia I can attest to many similar occurrences. I have learned that when one of my students risks sharing a painting, moving, writing poetry, or creating a performance in front of her peers it is important to receive a response from someone else in the group. We always give students the opportunity to select another person in the group to give an artistic response within the same medium. For example, if a student moves in response to her painting, she is asked to invite another member of the colloquium to give a response to her work. The peer selected to respond becomes a vital part of the process, and thus the focus is always on communal and shared expression rather than solo effort. The process of mutual response is, again, pleasurable and gratifying.

As the group members become immersed in this way of being with art they open themselves to the creative flow of the community and are less concerned about the potential negative interpretations their works might engender. In this way we get past the defensive stance and distrust of the aforementioned group critiques. As the colloquium weekend progresses a palpable artistic contagion is established that accentuates the pleasure and gratification of creative self-expression.

The discipline of reciprocal artistic response fosters immersion in present relationships with artworks and the people who created them that encourages creative expression to emerge spontaneously and rhythmically. I have engaged in similar interactions in clinical contexts, where groups are smaller and more intimate than the opening colloquium. In art-based therapy groups, often more than one person can respond to a client's artwork, and in these situations a cyclic phenomenon of creative expression is even more prominent and the variations of response are endless as one expression begets another, and another, and another.

McNiff (2009) emphasized that respondents must be free to relate to the artworks in whatever ways fit their sensibilities and imaginations. He stressed that artists like to see their works activate the imagination of another person and that artistic responses are the most affirming and personal thing that we can give a fellow group member. I want to emphasize that in the art-based therapy groups that I lead I try to liberate my clients from the concern that they have to give the "right" response to their fellow group members. They don't have to figure out what artists meant to express in their paintings and they don't need to come up with insightful psychological explanations of their responses to the works. It is much more important to respond genuinely from their own bodies and from the heart. I find that authentic responses, even those that may initially seem off base, are often the most emotionally compelling and have lasting influence on the recipient.

The reciprocal responses I have witnessed have taught me that what matters most in art-based therapy groups are the heartfelt expressions of support from one member to another. The process of responsive art making frequently becomes a life-changing experience of affirmation. I try to help clients realize that it is their generosity of response that forms the foundation of the therapeutic benefit to all in the group.

In my work with groups of adolescents and adults both within and outside of mental health settings, as well as with art therapy students, I have learned that the process of making art together and responding to artworks with another art form has a number of consistent positive effects. Responding to expressions that emerged in a person's art, or to feelings or problems experienced by individuals or groups, artistically helps people to move to another place and to alter their relationship to the artwork or feeling and transform it into a source of deeper expression. Rather than trying to explain our way out of a problematic feeling, we do something different with it and the creative response forms the foundation for a parallel change in self-awareness and feelings. Responsive art making becomes a vehicle for altering attitudes and behaviors.

This approach to art-based group therapy can alter how clients feel about difficult situations or problems in their lives by modeling different ways of relating to the issues, playing with them, and expressing and responding to them in various art forms without engaging in verbal analysis, formulaic interpretation, or explanation. The magic of such transformations is that they occur through creative processes that are often pleasurable and gratifying, even though their sources may be painful and difficult.

Chapter XI

SELF-TRANSCENDENCE

In art-based therapy groups, clients create meaning in their lives by being open to one another. Discovering personal meaning is not a private process. Frankl (1955) posited that meaning could only be found in self-transcendence, not self-actualization. He asserted, "self-actualization is possible only as a side effect of self-transcendence" (p. 133). In my work with clients I have learned that making art in a group setting is an act of self-transcendence. Artistic activities provide bridges from isolation to life with others. The visual arts serve as a transitional way to interact with other human beings in a context of self-expression and connection to others that can change clients' self images, build confidence, and facilitate becoming involved in a wider circle of human relationships. Art making engages clients in the world outside themselves. In art therapy groups, this transcendent absorption is a public act. Clients respond to the artworks of other clients. There is a contagious generosity that pervades the air of the art therapy studio.

In art-based group experiences, clients often find that their needs are best met as they give to others. In early stages of therapy, these same clients may feel isolated and empty, as if they have nothing of value to offer another human being. Still, through the processes of creating together and responding artistically, group members are able to offer tremendous support and help to each other. They serve as witnesses to one another's work, critique one another, share artistic techniques, make suggestions, and listen to and respond to one another. In my experience I have found that the relationships among clients formed in the context of art groups have at least as much to do with the eventual success or failure of the therapy as do their interactions with therapists.

An example of artistic self-transcendence was seen in Nancy's work in an art-based group. Nancy, a magazine editor in her mid thirties, had been in the group for several sessions. She was a precise, constricted, and rather remote woman. Although she had participated in the group activities, she had remained aloof from her peers. For this particular session I had taped large sheets of brown kraft paper on the walls of the group room and placed several boxes of pastel chalk on the floor. Addressing the members of the group, I said, "Today I want you to begin by putting your name at the top of the page and drawing seven circles on your paper." When everyone had done so, I then said, "I'd like us to move around the room to others' papers and draw lines, shapes, and colors that represent your impressions of that person in one of their circles."

Nancy reacted by commenting, "I don't think I can do that. I really don't know any of these people that well."

One of her peers replied, "C'mon, Nancy. You know me just as well as I know you."

"Give it a try, Nancy," I encouraged her. "There is no wrong way to do this. You don't have to think too much, just let yourself move in response to how you see the person. These are only first impressions and, again, there is no way to do it wrong. I'm sure that people are interested in how you see them."

Nancy seemed irritated by this and replied, "I'll just do the same thing on everyone's page then."

I said, "That will be fine, but maybe you could use colors too."

Nancy did not respond to that and after a moment group members began to move around the room and make their images of one another. When everyone, including Nancy, had finished we sat in a circle and began a discussion period. As group members looked at the images and talked about their visual representations of their impressions of one another, Nancy maintained her reserved stance and said very little. When it came time to discuss the images drawn on Nancy's page, an air of tension filled the small room.

Breaking the silence, Will said, "Well, I'll go. Nancy, I drew you as a steel girder. You seem so strong, it's like you don't ever bend."

Nancy did not respond verbally, but her body appeared to become more rigid and tense and she stared straight ahead as if bracing herself for an attack.

Patty asked, "Did you hear what Will said, Nancy?"

Nancy shifted uncomfortably in her chair and replied, "I heard him very clearly."

Referring to her drawing, Patty said, "I drew all those black hash marks. They are the same size and they are all in order, but there is something missing. I think there should be more."

Nancy reacted with, "I don't know what you mean."

Jerry spoke up. "My circle for you is that one filled with light brown. It blends in with the color of the paper. I wish I knew more about you, but I just couldn't think of anything."

Tears welled in Nancy's eyes, but she fought them.

Sherry said, "I drew the pile of books. You seem really intelligent but to me all the books are closed. I'd bet there are a lot of good stories, but I don't think I'd be allowed to read them."

Nancy turned away. In a gentle voice I said, "It's all right, Nancy. Let the tears come. Nobody here wants to hurt you, just let them come."

Nancy's tears came, and years of lonely sadness poured from her. Patty picked up a box of tissues and placed it beside her chair. She leaned over and gave her a hug.

After a few moments the group moved on to other pages and Nancy was able to offer her impressions more openly and authentically.

My group sessions have always been focused on the individual persons working in the presence of other group members who act as witnesses. We often work on similar artistic themes together as a group, but the sessions are usually organized so that everyone has the opportunity to express themselves before the group and also practice functioning as witnesses to others' work.

I have found that one of the most effective ways of supporting creative expression is to pay attention to how I (and others) witness and respond to what a person does within the art group. I emphasize that witnessing another person's artistic expression within a group can be just as important and active as expressing oneself. The active attention of each group member is needed to establish a milieu of reciprocal creative energy and expression.

The community of client-artists working together, paying attention to one another, and responding to each other's work establishes a tangible sense of creativity in art-based group work. This is an essential therapeutic quality of art-based group therapy and I have found that it also holds great appeal to clients who desire something other than traditional verbal group interaction. Clients participate in my groups in order to experience a sense of being part of something larger than themselves, where others accompany them on their journeys without harsh judgments and generously support them during periods of uncertainty and difficulty when they let go of typical patterns of relating in order to take their self-expressions to new and more genuine places.

Throughout history artists have demonstrated that creative expression can occur without the support of others, even in difficult times, and there are many who have used art as a way of coping who did not receive attention from others. In contrast to these private experiences of naturally occurring art therapy, the art therapy group experience is a context where other people will attend to and witness a client's expression. The role of group members is among the most essential components of the therapy group, perhaps even more important than that of the art therapist. When working with art-based groups the therapist enlarges the community of witnesses by demonstrating how to give creative attention to the expressions of others.

In my role as a leader I model and encourage focused attention as we witness another person working. I also offer clear guidelines for giving and receiving feedback, discouraging judgment and asking that group members respond to what they experience while compassionately observing their peers' artistic expressions. It is fascinating how group members' self-expressions can influence others, and enable others to be more effective in their own expression.

When a client's artistic expression disturbs or confuses a peer, the communication of this is encouraged as part of the natural give and take between artists and their audiences. I try to avoid comparing and critical judgments, intellectualized analyses, and psychological projections of "meanings" by group members. Rather, I encourage participants to describe how another person's art affects them and pay attention to the expressive characteristics of the experience, to comment respectfully, and to give responses that offer support and help to the artist.

In art therapy groups, clients meet their needs by giving to others. Sometimes the gifts are painful ones, and sometimes they are gentle and supportive. Clients often encourage one another and sometimes challenge. They share artistic and life strategies. They make aesthetic suggestions and listen to each other. Benevolence is the disposition to do good. It is seen in acts of kindness. Making art in the community of others is a self-transcendent and generous act, for it is a gift to others and an offering to life itself.

Chapter XII

ART-BASED GROUPS AND THE ULTIMATE CONCERNS OF EXISTENCE

People tend to come to art-based therapy groups when they are experiencing painful, disturbing, and difficult life crises. They seldom enter therapy in order to express how happy and fulfilled they are. The thorny events and situations that compel a person to seek art therapy are as diverse as the individuals themselves. Still, there are common concerns that appear time and again. These common themes are related to the ultimate concerns of existence: freedom, aloneness, guilt, personal responsibility for one's own life, the inevitability of suffering and death, and a longing for purpose and meaning.

In the art-based groups that I lead I have witnessed these existential concerns expressed innumerable times. In fact, I suspect that all art has an existential quality because artists throughout history have demonstrated that the creative impulse thrives in the face of hard times. For people entrenched in misfortune, artistic expressions and objects can give solace, support, and affirmation. Brought on by awareness of the ultimate concerns of existence, artists' personal difficulties and emotional turmoil often become a source for their creative work. The tradition of using art processes to grapple with the depths of human experience is an extraordinary gift that artist therapists can offer to the members of groups they lead. Artists have always struggled to express feelings and ideas related to personal meaning, isolation, death, and creative freedom.

From an existentialist perspective, people in therapy relate to these issues either by attempting to ignore them (denial) or by living in what Yalom (2005) referred to as a state of "mindfulness" (p. 104). Making art with others in a group setting helps clients to attune themselves to the ultimate concerns of existence and develop self-awareness. When leading groups, I encourage members to identify and express the meanings of their lives through artistic processes, products, and responses. I pay attention to the art processes and products that emerge in the context of relationships among clients and their expressions. A primary intention of the work in art-based groups is to engage the members in a creative effort to give form to the ultimate concerns of existence. A central concept, again, in using art processes in this way is that the artistic self-expression will lead individuals toward a state of mindfulness.

Working from this perspective I am more focused on encouraging the creative flow of group members' self-expression than on trying to determine causes of their problems and attempting to solve them. I believe that the essential concerns of our lives, both positive and negative, are a rich source of creativity. My intention is to help clients feel and express themselves more fully. It is surely true that most emotional problems cannot be reduced to single causes. The serious problems that bring people into therapy are typically complicated clusters of forces that are often difficult to isolate, but these forces can be channeled into artistic expressions that can alter situations and behaviors.

In my experience, the most genuine and transformative experiences in art-based groups occur when clients are able to work sequentially with their images and artworks. A client makes an image, another client responds artistically, and the artist makes again. In this way the original expression is reimagined and taken further, rather than given a fixed interpretation. The most authentic therapy happens when clients become immersed in the creative process. This way of working is in stark contrast to the more analytic and verbally dependent approaches that have been the hallmark of much of our art therapy group literature.

I believe that art making is a life-affirming impulse that is an expression of emotional health and vitality. As Prinzhorn (1922) described, "All expressive gestures as such are subordinated to one purpose: to actualize the psyche and thereby to build a bridge from the self to others" (p. 13). The desire to express one's self creatively is a life affirming instinct, and, as such, artistic expressions cannot avoid dealing with the ultimate concerns of existence. The images that emerge in art-based therapy groups enable the creator to reach beyond the bounds of his or her individual life circumstances and to experience the source of pleasure available in connecting with others in the group.

The practice of art-based therapy in groups is primarily concerned with helping people open themselves to the natural and healthy forces of artistic expression. I have mentioned earlier that many clients initially resist, fear, or question the value of making art. These adverse reactions are just as prevalent in art groups as are the healing potentials of artistic engagement. Still, my practice has taught me that the most troublesome problems—indeed the ultimate concerns of existence—are inextricably connected to art, and art can be used to express them in ways that affirm and support even the most disturbed clients.

Charles's Scriptures

Charles was a middle-aged man afflicted with chronic schizophrenia. When he was placed into Harding Psychiatric Hospital's art therapy group he was plagued by visual and auditory hallucinations. He rarely interacted with peers or members of the staff. Charles suffered from echolalia, which meant that when he did attempt to communicate, more often than not his speech was marked by involuntary parrot-like repetition of words or phrases. His movements were made stiff by psychotropic medications, he had a shuffling gate, and he seldom established eye contact. Although nearly always in the company of fellow clients and staff members, Charles was a living, breathing exception to John Donne's (1623/1999) rule that "No man is an island, entire of itself" (p. 103). Charles was certainly not part of the main.

He had been treated in a number of hospitals for many years prior to coming to Harding. His echolalia, isolation, and mannerisms gave the impression that he had severe developmental and intellectual limitations. But Charles's family records indicated that as a youth he had been an above average student, although he had been a shy child and a socially awkward adolescent. He'd received electroshock therapy in prior hospitalizations and this had seemed to increase his withdrawal.

He'd been coming to the creative arts building for a couple months, spending most of his time mumbling and arranging art supplies, disentangling boxes of yarn scraps, and other fairly menial tasks. There was some discussion among members of the activity therapy staff that Charles should be scheduled into another activity, perhaps horticulture, where he might find solace in the routine greenhouse maintenance tasks.

One afternoon in the studio, Charles sat looking out a window with his back to rest of the room. I was sitting next to him as he was sorting through an array of mosaic tiles, using a Popsicle stick to push them about, nudging the blue ones to the left side of the table, red to the right. I became interested in his process. The more intently I watched his hand motions, the more intrigued I became. His hand and stick moved swiftly but deliberately, and I sensed a quality of focus and attention to the job at hand that belied his typical distractedness.

"Charles, I've been watching and you are doing good work."

"Yes sir, the hand, the hand, the hand knows where they go."

That was all there was to our interaction that day. Charles continued to sort the tiles by color for the rest of the session. When it came time to leave he simply pushed all of the tiles back into the drawer they'd been in prior to his effort.

The mental image of Charles's deft movements and his concentration on the self-chosen task of sorting stuck with me throughout the day. I wondered if he could make those same motions with a pencil on paper, an oil stick on tagboard, or a paintbrush on canvas.

When Charles entered the building the next day he made his way to the table where he'd sat sorting mosaic tiles the previous day. Before he could become absorbed in the process of arranging tiles I approached and greeted him. "Charles, good to see you. How are you doing today?"

"Good day, good day . . . ready to work," he said.

"I have another job that you might like," I replied. I slid a large sheet of heavy drawing paper onto the table where he'd worked separating tiles.

"Do you remember using the stick yesterday to push those tiles around?"

"Yes sir, yes sir. Had to be done."

"Charles, I'd like for you to try to imagine moving the tiles around, only this time use a pencil to make marks on the paper."

"Don't see them," he said.

I responded, "That's all right. Just use your imagination and push them around."

Charles sort of half-grinned at me and said, "Push 'em around, push 'em . . . somebody has to."

Over the next two hours Charles exerted the same focus and attention to the task of using his pencil to sort unseen tiles onto opposite sides of the drawing paper: that is to say, he made marks. His ornamental and repetitive use of lines reminded me of works included in Prinzhorn's (1922) book, and they were reminiscent of drawings I'd seen in catalogs from *art brut* exhibitions. I believe that this resemblance was a manifestation of innate artistic patterns of expression whereby a composition is constructed by the simple and obsessive repeating of lines to form an overall pictorial design. I was fascinated by the way Charles formed a complex and visually interesting image while working so absorbedly. His drawing was aesthetically delightful and the repetition of lines gave quality of vitality mixed with tedium that was intriguing.

Charles's overt actions as he drew were reminiscent of his earlier sorting behavior, but the result was markedly different. His peers in the art therapy group noticed this change. They had grown accustomed to his verbal echoing and isolative, obsessive organizing. Charles's effort seemed to support Prinzhorn's notion that artists were spurred by an inherent desire for expression that in this case was made even more remarkable by Charles's interpersonal isolation from echolalia.

For the next few weeks, Charles worked several hours per day making intricate colored pencil drawings. Perhaps because traditional speech communication was not available to Charles, he turned to art and the spigot of self-expression was opened. His drawings and the process of making them provided an emotional outlet, a discipline of creative work, and connections with other people. His complex pictures intrigued other clients in the art studio and he was able to communicate with vigor and begin to form relationships.

One day, Ben, another client in the group, commented to Charles, "Your drawings seem so uninhibited. They look so free."

Without looking up from his work Charles responded, "Yes sir, freedom, freedom. Like a motherless child." After months of working in relative isolation, this was the first interaction with a peer in the group that I had observed.

Ben replied, "Oh man, I love Richie Haven's version of that song."

"Freedom, freedom . . . a long way from my home," Charles countered.

As I worked with Charles in the art therapy group there were many challenges, ebbs, and flows to the progress he was making. The unfolding of artistic self-expression is seldom a step-by-step process. But, over time, Charles gradually allowed more interactions with others into his lonely and constricted world. His artworks invariably referenced a mysterious connection with themes that seemed to echo the ultimate concerns of existence: aloneness, struggle, death, and an unspoken desire for meaning and connection to the larger world. In later works he frequently portrayed images of God, whom he referred to as the Lord Thorasia, and he illustrated private scriptures that seemed to reveal his view of the universe. Although he was unable to speak of these in ways that would be considered typical, his artworks clearly contained visual references to healing entities and there were noticeable changes in his energy level that had an impact on members of the immediate art studio community. In fact, his creative expressive work became a focal point of interaction for group members. Nearly everyone in the studio was interested in what he was doing, and what would come next. This fostered an air of creative contagion in the group that was truly remarkable.

As the months passed, a sense of comradeship developed as members of the group became increasingly interested in Charles's artistic expressions. As his peers responded to his drawings, and eventually his paintings, there was a shift in his overall demeanor in the studio and his ways of relating to others. The art group served as a kind of relational oasis where he began to be able to demonstrate capacities for creative expression and to initiate cautious connection to other people. In other areas of his life his withdrawal in relation to peers and hospital staff continued.

One of the most prominent features of this art-based group experience was the way in which Charles's drawings served as a catalyst of graphic emotional expression, not only for himself, but for others in the group as well. I believe that this was due to the unencumbered ways his images dealt with very complex life themes. His scriptural imagery clearly demonstrates how, even when he was totally withdrawn in terms of language and physical motion, he still felt a need to express existential concerns and feelings and transform experience symbolically through gestural drawings.

Mary Lou's Vision

Mary Lou, a 16-year-old, had been struggling with depression and anxiety since her parents' divorce. She had been referred to an art-based group for outpatients but had been a difficult client to engage with because she regularly skipped sessions, and when she did attend she complained loudly, to everyone in the group, that she was "B-O-R-E-D!"

My typical response to her grumbling was always the same: "Mary Lou, I believe that boredom comes from a lack of quality relationships. I wish you would let yourself not be bored here." Mary Lou would roll her eyes and scoff, "Oh God, you are so predictable. Do you have any idea how boring that is?" Her involvement in the group was marked by inconsistent attendance, a penchant for superfluous socializing, and cursory dabbling with art materials. So I was somewhat taken aback when she told me one afternoon that she wanted to try painting.

As I helped her build a frame and stretch the canvas I asked if she had a plan for the painting. "Mmm, sort of," she replied, "but I don't want to talk about it." The other adolescents in the group that day were, in varying degrees, down in the dumps, angry, and keyed up. One of the girls had had a difficult family therapy session earlier in the day. One client was excited in anticipation of a concert he was going to attend that weekend. Another girl was in tears over a nasty breakup with her boyfriend. So it was probably good that Mary Lou didn't want to talk too much about her plan.

She began by covering the canvas with swirls of dark red and black. Then she used bright blue paint to depict several abstract human figures placed randomly about the surface. For the first time in the group, Mary Lou immersed herself in making art and because there was so much going on with the other clients during the session I was not able to offer her too much attention. As we were putting away art materials and cleaning up the studio she approached me and asked quietly, "Before we leave today could we take a look at my painting?"

"Of course, Mary Lou. Let's get everything put away."

She replied, "I'm in no hurry today."

When everyone had cleaned up, the clients arranged their chairs in a circle and Mary Lou placed her painting on an easel. I said, "Yowsa, Mary Lou, no boredom today."

She looked at me. "No. No boredom, but I'm not really sure what to say about it. It's hard."

"Sometimes nothing needs to be said. In our group I think just making art and expressing yourself in that way is most important."

She sighed. "You really are so predictable. I've heard you say stuff like that enough times."

Another client, Tegan, chimed in, "Haven't we all."

"I just want you to know that your art is important here."

"Yeah, I know. But I want to." She paused. "This is a picture about my family. They are all over the place. Nobody is looking at the others." She began to cry. "I used to think. . . ." More tears. Tegan reached for the box of tissues on the counter and offered it to Mary Lou.

"I know I've been a pain in the butt in this group," she sniffled.

"It's okay. I know that being in therapy is hard. Nobody really wants to do it. I am used to kids not having their best days here."

She gestured toward her painting again. "When I was little it seemed like we were the perfect family."

Another client, Leah, responded, "My parents split up too. I remember thinking the same thing. We had a perfect house, perfect cars, and a perfect dog. Everything was perfect, until . . . it wasn't."

Mary Lou said, "When things got bad they'd get into these awful fights. Scream and call each other horrible names. My dad told me I had to choose sides." Her body shook with tears. "It makes me feel sick inside."

Tegan said, "You've been through some real crap." The group sat quietly for a few moments. Mary Lou wrapped her arms tightly against her body.

I said, "Your painting really gets at the feelings of isolation and separation, Mary Lou. Even though it is hard for you to look at, I think it is perfect just the way it is. But if you could change it somehow, what would you do?"

"These people," she said, pointing. "I wish they'd turn around and look at each other. All I want is for them to hold me. Or maybe I just want them to leave me alone."

Leah reached over and gently placed her hand on Mary Lou's shoulder.

Mary Lou said, "This hurts so bad. Sometimes I just want to hurt everybody else."

In an exquisite moment of compassion, Tegan slowly rose from her chair, faced Mary Lou, and covered her heart with both hands. She moved her hands gently, as if they were in rhythm with her pulse. She then extended her arms toward Mary Lou, symbolically offering her heart.

Speaking softly to the group I said, "There are days when I am amazed by things that happen in this group. The kindness I see you offer to one another . . . it is an honor for me to be with here with you." The group was quiet and still.

I went on, "As you know, I think artworks are sort of like partial self-portraits. Painting is like life. If you don't like what you've done, you can back up and change the picture if you want to."

Mary Lou dabbed her eyes and gave me a skeptical look. "What is that supposed mean?"

"You can change the painting, Mary Lou. In your art, you're the boss. You can change the canvas any way you want. You can paint over the figures, or make them all holding hands, or at least looking toward one another—anything you want."

She considered the possibilities for a moment, but then said, "No, this is the way it is right now. We are all alone. But maybe I'll do another painting of us next week. You never know what might happen in families."

In the months that followed, Mary Lou created several paintings of her family, and she made an exquisite sculpture of a bird's nest holding four eggs in various stages of cracking and opening. Sometimes she talked with the group about what her artworks meant to her, sometimes she just made them and then moved on. My work with art-based therapy groups has taught me how important it is to offer clients a stage upon which they can create artworks that represent the way their lives are, and begin to imagine the way their lives can be. This is work that people cannot do alone. We accompany.

The relationship between art making and existential ultimate concerns is unavoidable. When we are able to help group members honestly come to grips with and do something creative with their burdens and fears, they experience ways of being in the group that are noticeably different from the patterns of behavior that occur when these afflictions and insecurities are denied and suppressed. Similarly, it is important to encourage clients to experiment and embrace ways of self-expression that they may have not previously valued. Again, an essential part of the transformational process in art-based groups involves engaging group members to creatively respond to one another. Tegan's enactment of giving her heart was a truly profound expression of community that no words could have conveyed.

I confess, there was a time when my professional self-esteem was based on my capacity to know the meanings of client's work, whether they knew them or not. Now I am much more likely to stand before their images (and my own) in an attitude of wonder, and a sense of not knowing. As one client said to me, "I don't know what my artwork means, but I know it has meaning."

The most effective therapeutic art groups acknowledge and embrace the difficulties and pain of self-expression. It is entirely natural for our clients to resist engaging in creative expression even as they long for the relief that self-expression brings. The safest and most transformative art milieus recognize that the creative process needs darkness together with light, and both villainous and heroic forces. Art's transformative powers are comprised of both medicinal and toxic elements. All of these ingredients contribute to the alchemical stew of art-based group therapy.

An important characteristic of the expression of existential concerns in art is an acceptance of the role of creative deconstruction and artistic reintegration in the company of others. Perhaps one of the most distinguishing features of art-based group work is support for authentically taking stock of the way things are in life, and, in a sense, falling apart in order to transform our lives and existential conditions. Disturbing and upsetting creative expressions do not fluster well-functioning art groups. Even when I am sometimes caught off guard or made uneasy by an expressive form, I keep learning how these potent and often repressed forces can be engaged in the arts to help shake up destructive patterns of behavior and thinking that intrude and limit clients' lives.

Existentialism has often been misrepresented as a philosophy marked by anguish. People often find themselves so distracted by existentialist authors' skepticism and rejection of familiar and traditional values that they fail to grasp the subtle, yet constant, undertones of hope. Existentialists' doubts that human beings can find self-fulfillment through wealth, fame, or pleasure is often perceived as cold detachment, bitterness, and despair. Their embrace of the notion that all life is marked by suffering and loss derides customary attempts to achieve happiness. The existentialist proposition that pain, frustration, guilt, and anxiety are unavoidable can be challenging. Those who see the existentialists' embrace of these "life realities" often fail to see the accompanying belief that striving generates truly authentic and admirable values.

I hope that the art therapy professional community will come to fully appreciate the existential dimensions of art-based group work. At their best, art therapy groups can be sanctuaries of creative self-expression and integration, places where clients are supported and inspired to take risks and to give form to feelings and ideas that provide the basis for acceptance and transformation of the deep concerns of their lives.

Chapter XIII

LOOKING IN THE MIRROR WITH OTHERS

In the early stages of graduate school, my students are often so filled with enthusiasm, excitement, and awe regarding the healing power of art making that there is a tendency to romanticize art therapy practice. Although I always appreciate students' energy and optimism, I also remind them that no one comes into therapy because of their good feelings. On the contrary, clients come to art therapy because of broken, wounded, and disturbing feelings they bear. Depending upon the nature of the treatment setting, some clients enter art-based therapy groups voluntarily, whereas those in other settings may be compelled to participate. Regardless of how or why clients are referred to art-based groups, it is imperative that group leaders be mindful of the fact that expressing the feelings associated with emotional and psychological wounds is seldom easy for people. In fact, expressing such feelings initially may lead to even more discomfort and distress.

In *Existential Art Therapy* (B. Moon, 2009) I used the metaphor of a canvas mirror to describe the process of artistic self-expression.

> As artists create they struggle with their conscious and unconscious depths to free images and give them life on the canvas. The canvas mirror reflects many realities simultaneously: present, past, and future. . . .When artists have looked into the canvas mirror and allowed the flow of imagery from self to proceed, they have said in the most honest of ways: "This is who I am. This is why I am." (p. 114)

It is not easy to look honestly into the mirror.

For art-based group leaders, the purpose of exploring difficult feelings through art is not to assume the role of an expert who can then advise the client but rather to become a fellow traveler who can be fully present alongside the suffering of another individual. Through this authentic presence and struggling in the studio in full view of others, the art therapist models the belief that the struggle is worth it: that breaking out of the numbing cocoon that separates people from their pain is worthwhile, necessary, even joyful at times, if people allow themselves to be fully alive. After all, through brokenness, people can connect with others, and that is how meaning is created.

In the case of physical injuries, we know that pain serves an important function by letting us know that something is wrong. In my life I have broken my heel, my jaw, and the fifth metatarsal bones in both of my feet. Each time I broke a bone, there was an immediate pain signaling that something was wrong and needed attention. After awhile the pain would diminish, and as I would lie in emergency room bed awaiting the results of the x-rays, I could almost convince myself that no bone was broken. Then the doctor would enter the room and deliver the bad news. Every time, the physician had to realign the bone so that it could heal properly. Setting the bone always reignited the pain of the break. For clients, entering an art-based therapy group can be a little like setting a broken bone, and despite the good intentions of art therapists, clients cannot help but associate them with the pain of life. Clients come bearing complex and painful emotions that include low self-esteem, powerlessness, shame, guilt, fear, embarrassment, betrayal, and rage.

Making art with others is a safe way to express the painful, frightening, and difficult feelings that are connected to emotional wounds. Artistic expression and healing are inseparable. As McNiff (2003) noted:

> Healing is different from curing. Whereas the latter eradicates symptoms, the former involves attitudinal changes, learning how to live with problems and even to use them in some creative way. Healing also entails accepting the conditions of our lives, appreciating what we have, letting go of complaints, realizing that we are not alone in our difficulties, and feeling connected to the whole of experience. (p. 214)

Some therapists view their role as alleviating clients' discomfort. But I take a different view. When I am leading art-based groups I do not try to help clients feel better; rather, I try to help them express their feelings in ways that lead to new understandings of the meanings of their distress. Often, this help clients feel more at ease, less anxious, and less in pain, but that is a coincidental side effect of participating in the art therapy group–the icing on the cake. By honoring clients' feelings and not trying to mask or get rid of them, I provide a milieu in which clients are free to feel intensely whatever they feel. Paradoxically, this often results in clients feeling better. An essential aspect of art-based group work is the art therapist's belief that uncomfortable feelings should not be eliminated but rather embraced and understood. The capacity of art therapists to accept clients' feelings hinges on their attitudes toward their own feelings.

In art-based therapy groups I have always told clients that I do not regard feelings as good or bad, or positive or negative. Feelings are just feelings. I liken feelings to energy, which, again, is neither good nor bad. Although it is true that people can use energy for good purposes or for evil purposes, the energy itself is merely neutral potential.

In the same way, I model acceptance of all images that arrive in the group context. Clients' images can often be disturbing, and sometimes therapists attempt to censor or bowdlerize them. I prefer to welcome all images, to make room for them and give them time to tell their stories. "Art does not profess to rid the world of suffering and wounds. . . . The big transitions are rarely planned and arrive in their own time, often contradicting the artist's intention" (McNiff, 2004, p. 32). Healing happens among group members when we are open to the messages of images and able to be present with them, rather than attempting to fix or resolve their discontents.

As difficult and painful as looking into the emotional mirror of artistic self-expression can be, it is true that art and emotional conflict have been closely allied for a long time. A character in Stephen King's (1988) novel *Misery* describes the relationship of art and emotional turmoil this way:

> Because writers remember everything, Paul. Especially the hurts. Strip a writer to the buff, point to the scars and he'll tell you the story of each small one. From the big ones you get novels, not amnesia. A little talent is a nice thing to have if you want to be a writer, but the only real requirement is that ability to remember the story of every scar.
>
> Art consists of the persistence of memory. (p. 219)

The purpose of art is to transform the scars of life: to use painful and disturbing experiences as the source material of creative expression.

This transformation represents and makes sacred the polarities and realities in people's lives. It allows artists to synchronize with the natural flow of life.

The Story of Darien

When I first met Darien, she was in intense emotional distress. She was admitted to the psychiatric hospital after becoming withdrawn and isolated for several months. She had retreated to the confines of her small one-room apartment. Darien had a well-documented history of problematic behavior, including episodes of unprovoked aggression toward others, self-mutilation by cutting, and other concerning behaviors. She complained of visual hallucinations and hearing voices, and she'd been hospitalized several times in the past few years.

As Darien grew more comfortable and trusting of the hospital staff, she described events from her life that underscored the severity of her illness, as well as thoughts she'd had. Darien experienced periods of dissociation and intrusive delusional thoughts. Darien's psychiatrist and members of the nursing staff were concerned about her inability to function in activities on the unit. She spent a great deal of time alone in her room. Her inability to manage her thoughts and impulses made it difficult to involver her in activities that included relating to other people.

During a treatment team discussion about these concerns, I suggested that we consider asking Darien if she would be willing to participate in one of the art-based therapy groups that I led. This suggestion was contrary to the treatment team's philosophy that creative expression was not helpful to people suffering with thought disorders. My fellow team members were concerned that artistic self-expression would stimulate disturbing feelings and impulses that would lead clients to feel even more unstable than they already felt. Although I appreciated the concerns that other team members held because of this theoretical perspective, I countered that art can also be a transformative and structuring process that could be very helpful to Darien. This assertion caused a fair amount of internal debate. Eventually the psychiatrist interceded, saying that he would keep my suggestion in mind, but for the present, the treatment plan would proceed based on the general philosophy of the team.

Over the next two weeks, Darien's withdrawal worsened and she became even more isolative. At another treatment team meeting, members expressed concern for how little contact she was having with her peers and the staff. As the discussion proceeded, one of the psychiatric aids said that he had noticed Darien drawing in her room from time to time, and he'd found several sketches in her wastebasket. This rekindled the idea of using art as a way to relate with her. Although the psychiatrist still had concerns that artistic expression might "loosen her already shaky ego-boundaries," he suggested that we try entering her into the art therapy group.

Later that day I approached Darien as she sat alone at a card table in the day room. I introduced myself and said, "I am an artist and I have heard that you like to draw." She did not look up from the table, but mumbled a brief response. I told her that I was interested in seeing her work if she wanted to share it. I went on, "I run an art group that meets twice a week in the creative arts studio. I wonder if you'd like to join us?"

Darien asked, "What do they do in the group?"

"What each person does is really up to the individual artist. The group meets for an hour and a half, and we usually spend most of our time just making art, but we often talk about our work too . . . you know, what we are trying to express, that sort of thing."

She looked up and her face seemed to brighten a bit. "I could try that," she said.

Darien attended her first art-based group session the following Tuesday. She entered the studio hesitantly, as if she was afraid. I welcomed her and invited her to take a chair in our circle for the opening ritual of checking in with each group member. When her turn came to say how she felt that day, Darien kept her eyes focused on the floor and said, "I don't really know what to say, but I like art so I guess I am glad to be here." After everyone had checked in, Marla, another member of the group, offered to show Darien around the studio and help her get oriented as to where the various materials were kept. I watched as Marla and Darien moved around the studio. Marla pointed out features of the space, sometimes greeted another member of the group, sometimes said something that made Darien smile. Although Darien by no means initiated much in the way of social interaction, she did, in fact, relate with Marla. This was already a marked contrast to her isolative behavior on the unit.

When Marla had completed the studio tour, I asked Darien what she would like to do.

"I want to paint," she said.

"That's fine: there are a number of options. You can paint on a canvas board, or Masonite panel, or we can build a frame and stretch a canvas. What would you prefer?"

"I've used canvas boards before . . . so that would be good."

Within minutes Darien had gathered several jars of acrylic paint, brushes, and a container of water, and begun to work. From time to time I have had colleagues from verbally oriented helping professions suggest that if clients' experiences are not put into words, then no real therapeutic change has occurred. Although Darien did not engage in the social banter that occurred among other group members, she was not alone, and she was engaged with materials. There is probably nothing more important than getting started, touching brushes to paint, and applying paint to the surface. In addition, seven or eight other artists—her peers and I—surrounded her, and an almost palpable, yet invisible, force permeated the studio.

Creative activity has much in common with alchemy in that it is based upon the interactions of different elements. In the art studio, creative energy surged among the artists' movements, materials, images, interpersonal connections, and interactions. Art-based group therapy encourages clients to create from the difficult places of their lives with a deep faith that artistic processes will succeed in transforming disturbing images from the mirror into something new.

A little more than an hour had passed when I invited the group members to circle up in order to share what they had been working on with their peers. When everyone had gathered, Jessica, a young woman struggling with depression, volunteered to begin. She had created an image of a bleak and barren landscape in black and muddy gray-brown. She said, "I am not sure why I painted this, it just came to my mind. As I look at it now, though, it sorta reminds me of how things are."

I responded, "Jessica, I think that images come to us for a reason. Like they want to tell us something."

She looked doubtful. "Hmm, maybe this painting is telling me that I should just give up," she said sarcastically. Several of her peers laughed at her irony.

I said, "It looks like a lonely place." Addressing the other group members, I asked, "If one of you was out walking and came to this place, what would you do?"

Tom, a man in his fifties, answered, "It doesn't look like much is happening there. I think I'd just keep going."

Jane, a college student, chimed in, "I think it looks kinda boring."

Marla said, "If I was there I think I'd feel lonely.

As these words left Marla's lips, Darien's facial expression shifted from her habitual flatness to a hesitant hint of a smile. She said, "I think it looks like a good place—no one there to bother you, or hurt you."

Jessica audibly sighed. I asked if she wanted to say anything more about her image. She quietly said, "No."

Darien then placed her painting on the floor in front of her (see Figure 8 & Plate 8). She did not say anything.

Jessica reacted by saying, "Darien, I really like all the layers and the textures in your work."

Tom said, "It looks pretty rough."

Darien did not respond.

Marla offered, "I don't know what your painting means, Darien, but it sure looks like it means something. I mean, just visually, it works for me."

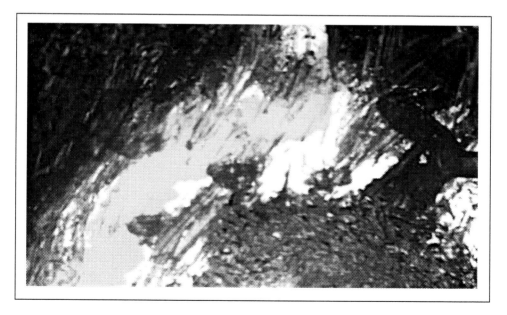

Figure 8. Darien's First Painting

When everyone had had a chance to say something (or nothing) about their artworks, and we had cleaned up the studio, I watched through the window as Darien, Marla, and Jessica walked back toward the unit together. I have no idea what they were talking about, but they were talking.

Darien attended many more art therapy group sessions and created a number of very interesting, yet hard to describe, paintings. Gradually, she created artworks that were more explicitly related to feelings and she and her peers sometimes talked more directly about feelings they shared—pain, fear, sadness, loneliness, and anger. More times than not, however, Darien preferred to work as long as possible during sessions and talk as little as possible.

For many clients, being in an art-based therapy group can be quite difficult. Most often entry into a group is initiated because the client is in crisis. The specific events and circumstances that lead people to seek art therapy are as diverse as the individuals themselves. Artists have always known that the principal source of their creative work is the emotional disquiet brought on by their struggle with life circumstances. A central tenet of art-based group work is that people relate to these issues either by attempting to ignore them or by living in Yalom's (2005) state of mindfulness. With clients like Darien, making art with others offers a safe way to express the painful, frightening, and difficult feelings that emanate from unspeakable emotional wounds.

Artistic expression and healing are inseparable. The work is tied to the creative struggle with the core issues of meaning, isolation, freedom, and death. The heart of art-based group therapy is found in artworks and visual images that emerge as expressions of these concerns. The work of an art-based group leader can be thought of as going on a shared artistic journey with clients. The purpose of the journey is to explore the meanings and themes of clients' lives as they emerge in artistic processes and products, and through group interaction. Art therapy group leaders ought not act as an interpreters or diagnosticians; rather, they should encourage clients to make their own interpretations and become immersed in the creative flow of expression and interpersonal sharing.

Chapter XIV

GROUP LEADERSHIP

Philosopher William Ockham is best remembered for the maxim attributed to him and known as *Occam's razor*. The term *razor* refers to the act of cutting away unnecessary assumptions in order to get to the simplest explanation of phenomena. I have found this aphorism helpful in relation to group leadership. I strive to keep things simple in terms of what I initiate in my groups, and then to be as sensitive and adaptable as possible in responding to the boundless forms of expression that arise as people make and respond to art. There was a time in my career when I felt it was necessary for me to be actively in charge of sessions, but I have learned the importance of moderation in leadership. I try to be carefully attentive to individual group members and their artworks, while at the same time encouraging others to respond to their peers' work in creative ways.

I have also learned that it is important to keep asking fundamental questions and to be flexible and open to change in leadership practices. In my career I have evolved and made significant shifts in how I begin group sessions, how much structure I provide, how I use my art making in sessions, how I deal with the pain and angst of clients, and how I take care of myself. No doubt I will continue to alter my practices and experiment in an effort to become more effective in helping others.

There are aspects of group leadership that have been difficult for me over the course of my career. I struggle with how some clients resist expressing themselves creatively and then project their discomfort and difficulties onto me. Like all art group leaders I want to be helpful to clients, so their occasional hostility toward the work takes me aback and, even though I understand it, I am never entirely comfortable with it. Still, I have learned that negativity and other difficult emotions are essential to the work that occurs in art-based therapy groups. It is natural for people to initially feel defensive when encouraged to express themselves in unfamiliar and self-revealing ways that are outside their comfort zone. The same thing applies to my experience over the years in leading student groups. The best results occur when I am able to see, listen, and be receptive to group members when they take the risk of expressing uncomfortable feelings. Art-based group leadership demands working with difficult feelings in the service of artistic self-expression.

My mentor Don Jones often urged me to "seek anxiety." He assured me that conflict is inevitable, particularly for those who would be group leaders. If we want to work closely with others' disturbances through the creative process, we must accept turmoil and put it to use. As a group leader I try to remain open to the dissonance and friction that inevitably arise in sessions; to take them in and be with them. But I cannot simply take in the toxins of clients' emotions. I have to make my own art in order to discharge and transform the negative energy and to allow it to pass through me.

As we work with people who are suffering from emotional and mental disturbances, physical traumas, or life altering diseases—the discounted and disenfranchised—we come into intimate contact with incredibly painful and difficult life stories. As group leaders we cannot avoid being moved by our clients and dare not shield ourselves from our own powerful feelings. Yet we cannot afford to be overwhelmed or vicariously traumatized by our clients either. I tell my students, "It really is like playing guitar—a guitarist has to have calluses in order to tolerate the pressure of the strings on his or her fingers, but the calluses cannot be so thick that the player can't feel the strings." I believe that one of the most effective ways for art therapists to build appropriate calluses and soothe the pain of unavoidable psychic blisters is through making their own art. Making art provides a healthy, practical, and authentic mechanism for art therapists to tend to the self, to ensure professional survival.

As a leader, I let group members' stories and images impact me and then I respond to them artistically, which in turn deepens my understanding and empathy. After many years in leadership positions within clinical and educational settings, I can vouch for the therapeutic value of being empathically moved by the struggles of clients. When I am a member of a group, I appreciate leaders who are able to creatively work with turmoil, who do not keep themselves aloof from the feelings of others, and who do not pretend to have easy formulas for the resolution of problems. For me, the challenge of remaining open to whatever emerges in the creative process helps to sustain my interest and involvement in group work.

There are extraordinary moments when amazing, life-changing things happen for clients, but in general the practice of art-based leadership is seldom easy. I get concerned when a group is running too smoothly. The work of creative self-expression and transformation is hard and often accompanied by elements of struggle, angst, and resistance. Clients come to art-based therapy groups in order to deal with dark, uncertain, and troubling issues. When a group is too positive, or too easy to work with, I always wonder what feelings are being avoided or denied by the members.

My work in psychiatric hospitals and residential treatment programs has pushed me to think deeply about my identity as a group leader. Like many in art therapy, during training I was indoctrinated with images of the selfless, unconditionally accepting, and neutral therapist. Such images have been handed down from Freud in the form of the "blank slate," and from Roger's (1951) notion of the therapist as alter ego, "a self which has temporarily divested itself of its own selfhood" (p. x). These are fine ideas and they may make a lot of sense when working with articulate and sophisticated clients who are capable of insight.

These theories have manifested themselves in art therapy in any number of ways. In no particular order some of these manifestations are: (a) the idea that the therapist ought not comment on the aesthetic merit of client work, (b) the belief that art therapists should avoid physical contact with clients' artworks, (c) the precept that therapeutic opacity equals appropriate professional boundaries, and (d) the tenet that art therapists should not make art alongside clients because that would contaminate the purity of clients' expressions.

My experiences working with client groups in hospitals and residential treatment centers where clients struggle to be articulate, are often unsophisticated, and more times than not are actively resistive have pushed me to revisit and revise my thinking about therapeutic personae. In such environments I have often seen examples of how I do not want to behave. Some therapists have adopted an approach that might best be described as "unconditional negative regard."

Others seem to live by the motto, "When in doubt, punish." Still others manifest what I call the "Casper Quality": that is, they remind me of ghosts—evasive, elusive, and impossible to touch. In my view none of these approaches are particularly helpful to clients. Those in the *unconditional negative regard* camp never believe a thing the clients say. The *when in doubt, punish* practitioners continually convey messages that the clients are bad and really should be incarcerated rather than in treatment. Those in the *ghost* camp are perhaps theoretical descendants of therapeutic neutrality, and although they are not as overtly harmful as the tow groups above, they keep themselves so hidden from their clients that it is as if they are not even there.

In my teaching I do not encourage formulaic approaches to group leadership and I expect students to experiment with their own therapeutic styles. This is often counter to students' desire for cookbook instructions that lead to rote leadership strategies and techniques. I expect students to become fully immersed in the creative process and to utilize their own experiences and understandings. Still, even the most gifted and innovative students find it natural to resist entering into the emotional chaos that accompanies self-expression and personal artistic inquiry.

Personal Characteristics of Leaders

Art therapy group processes cannot be detached from the leader's personal behaviors and qualities. The successes or failures, in terms of therapeutic outcomes, of art groups are integrally connected to the leadership skills of the art therapist. In art-based group therapy it is essential that the group leader constantly work to foster artistic contagion and to develop consistent and positive relationships among group members. The overt, but unspoken, attitude of art therapy group leaders must include concern, acceptance, and willingness to engage with clients in their pain and creative risk-taking as they struggle to find meaning in their lives. Corey (2004) noted, "the most effective group direction is found in the kind of life the group members see the leader demonstrating and not in the words they hear the leader saying" (p. 25).

In my work I have found that clients are inspired by the artistic commitment, passion, and enthusiasm of the group leader. Group members most easily observe the group leader's enthusiasm in his or her artistic work. In the course of group sessions, when art therapists are actively engaged in artistic self-expression a metaverbal air of positive creativity evolves in the group that is powerful medicine. Establishing this sense of artistic contagion is entirely the responsibility of the group leader. Art therapists simply cannot expect a group of suffering people to generate artistic vitality of their own accord. Although there are exceptions, most clients who seek therapy do not feel positively about themselves or others, and therefore cannot be expected to be enthusiastic artists. In my experience, the clients most often referred to art-based therapy groups tend to be depressed, angry, hurt, and unenthusiastic individuals, so the creation of artistic infectiousness is the group leader's responsibility.

In the context of group settings, artistic contagion is stimulated by the art therapist's ongoing commitment to making art. This is not necessarily talked about, but rather is acted out in the group milieu. The art therapist uses tone of voice, facial expressions, body movements, energy level, personality, and charisma in order to convey creative fervor in the group. My experience in art-based groups has taught me that it is essential for art therapists to exude a good amount of excitement, expectation, and joy in their work, while at the same time being able to honor and respect the discomfort, pain, sadness, and angst that group members often experience.

Corey (2004) listed eight personal characteristics that he deemed vitally related to effective group leadership: presence, personal power, courage, willingness to confront oneself, sincerity and authenticity, a sense of identity, belief in the group process and enthusiasm, and inventiveness and creativity (p. 26). There is no single ideal personality type for art-based group leaders. Some group leaders are outgoing extraverts, some are quietly gentle, and there are countless variations in between. However, it is imperative that art therapists develop the capacity to be truly attentive to group members–to really be with them. Moustakas (1995) described what I consider to be the essence of *therapeutic presence* for art therapy group leaders when he discussed *Being-In, Being-For,* and *Being-With* (pp. 155-158). *Being-In* requires that the art therapist enter into group members' artistic expressions exactly as they are given. When the leader therapist is able to genuinely *Be-In* the client's imagery world, the person feels understood. The leader's *Being-For* task is to actively encourage the artistic expressions that facilitate self-actualization. The art therapist not only accepts the artworks as presented, but is clearly and solidly regarded as an ally. This of course entails making available artistic resources, technical experience, competencies, and skills to group members so that they can effectively express themselves. The *Being-With* process involves the creation of an *I-Thou* relationship among the group members. The process facilitates very positive moments when the group members and leader are working together as a team.

Art therapists also need to have a sense of personal power and self-confidence if they want to be effective group leaders. This means that leaders must work with their unique personality traits and develop therapeutic styles that emanate healthy leadership personae. Therapeutic styles may take many forms. I have observed leaders who were able to fill up a room with their calm authenticity. Others are able to create a dynamic atmosphere through their gregarious warmth and energy.

Effective leaders of art-based therapy groups serve as artistic role models. As such, they must demonstrate a willingness to take both personal and creative risks. They allow themselves to be vulnerable and to relate authentically with the members of the group. Two of the primary tasks of group work are to promote self-expression and self-investigation in clients. Art therapists cannot ask group members to do something that they would not do themselves, thus group leaders have to demonstrate a willingness to explore and question themselves through artwork.

An underlying intention of group leaders is to accompany clients as they engage in creative self-expression. Art therapists want to artistically, behaviorally, and verbally convey the message that clients' expressions of feelings have value. One of the leader's most important qualities is a genuine interest in the growth and well-being of others. This entails a willingness to be compassionately direct, open, and honest with group members.

In order to relate in an authentic manner, art-based group leaders must wrestle with questions regarding the extent of our transparency with clients. What should we share about our lives with the group? How closely should we guard our personal privacy? When and why do we share personal information with clients? What are our professional boundaries? These questions help us to focus on the issues of openness between group leaders and group members.

OPAQUENESS	TRANSLUCENCE	TRANSPARENCY
The group leader does not make art in the company of clients. All aspects of the leader's life are withheld from group members.	The group leader uses his/her art making in a thoughtful manner and is cautious and selective about sharing personal information with the group. The leader always asks him-or herself how his/her artistic and relational self-disclosure will be helpful to the group.	The group leader always makes art in the company of clients and does not filter or censor his/her artistic expressions. The art-based group is viewed as a context for mutual exchange of self-expressions among group members and the leader.

In relation to the issues of leaders' artistic and relational self-disclosure, there is a continuum ranging from complete opaqueness to transparency, with translucence approximately midway between:

Art therapists must decide for themselves where their leadership styles fall on this continuum. When my students ask me for "the rules" regarding proper professional behavior in relation to self-disclosure in groups, I respond by saying that they must experience the emptiness of a missed opportunity when they unnecessarily withhold information. Likewise, they must feel the pain of being hurt by the client who was not ready or able to respond positively to the gift of the group leader's vulnerability. These feelings must be experienced time and again to develop a set of inner cues that encourage one to reveal and warn one to withhold. Regardless of the level of self-disclosure that group leaders choose, it is essential that self-awareness remains a top priority. To maintain our authenticity as art therapists, we must be willing to constantly look in the creative mirror. We may on occasion need to be opaque to our clients, but we can never be less than transparent to ourselves.

In other publications I have recounted the story of a whitewater rafting adventure I had with my wife and friends on the New River in West Virginia. As we entered the second rapid, I was thrown out of the raft. Although my life preserver did its job and I made it through the rapid without a scratch, I was shaking internally. The whitewater was so overpowering that there was no way for a swimmer to have control; all I could do was go with the flow.

When we stopped for lunch later in the day, the head guide climbed up on a large boulder on the riverbank and told us in great detail how to make a peanut butter and jelly sandwich. As silly as that sounds, the psychological effect was wonderful. He was in control: not wet and not frightened. I found it reassuring to be told how to make sandwiches. He gave order to the swirling chaos of that morning on the river.

For clients, joining an art therapy group is usually an indicator of the level of turmoil and emotional whitewater they have been experiencing. It is a symbolic acknowledgment that the struggle and discomfort of the therapeutic journey is necessary. Just as I needed the river guide to be calm and in control—he had been down this river before—groups need their leaders to have a clear sense of their own self-identities.

Art-based group leaders must have a deep belief in art processes and in the healthiness of creative self-expression. By this I mean that we must have faith in the goodness of life, the arts, others, and ourselves. Fromm (1956) said that only people who have faith in themselves are able to be faithful to and trustworthy of others. I would suggest that only group leaders who have faith in their own art processes and products are able to have faith in those of their clients. Without a belief in the power of images and artworks to heal, we have no reason to be art-based group leaders. "The best way to lead others is to demonstrate what you believe through your own life" (Corey et al., 2008, p. 28). Art therapists who want to lead groups, ultimately, must walk the walk of artistic self-expression in the service of relationships.

Yalom (2005) described three basic leadership tasks of verbal psychotherapy group therapists. The first is the creation and maintenance of the group. The second is culture building, wherein therapists establish a code of behavioral rules to guide the group's interaction. The third is keeping the focus of the group in the here and now. Art-based group leaders have responsibilities similar to those Yalom outlined for verbal therapists. First, art therapists set up the time and frequency of sessions, provide art materials, and maintain the studio space. Second, art therapists shape the cultural norms of their groups. For example, in my practice I make sure that sessions begin and end on time. Being punctual and ready to get to work at the prescribed time conveys a powerful implicit message. Group members learn through observation that I value our time together, and the culture is built and reinforced by my modeling. Clients' willingness to take risks and actively involve themselves in creative self-expression is directly influenced by art therapists' enthusiasm and work ethic. The third task for art-based group leaders is to keep the focus of group members on artistic self-expression and creative response to one another. In practice, my investment in art processes, belief in the power and goodness of creative self-expression, willingness to respond authentically to group members' images, and openness to whatever clients create set the tone of the group.

In my work with students who want to become group leaders, I emphasize that the basic functions of leadership are relatively simple: (1) hold the space, (2) create a culture of artistic contagion, and (3) encourage safety and predictability in the group. When I discuss these functions of group leadership I am referring to leaders' efforts to attend to: (a) the overall ambiance of the studio or group room, (b) the range of art materials and equipment, (c) the rituals of beginning, immersing, and ending sessions, (d) the furniture, floor plan, and organization of the space, (e) the presence (or absence) of music, (f) the rules of behavior, (g) the privileges and restrictions that are associated with the use of specific tools or materials, (h) the creative enthusiasm of the leader, and (i) the stability, consistency, and reliability of the leader. Added together, these functions and qualities serve as a container for group members' feelings, ideas, behaviors, and relationships. In an art-based therapy group the overall ambiance, the essence of the place, emerges in the interactions of people, images, and the environment, while simultaneously transforming them. Another way to think of the structure of the therapeutic arts studio is that it is the sum of all of the overt and covert elements of the artistic milieu.

In *A Sense of Place*, Gussow (1971) wrote that the thing that changes any physical location into *a place* is the process of experiencing deeply. "A place is a piece of the whole environment that has been claimed by feelings" (p. 27). Artworks on the walls of a studio or group room can have compelling influence on the feel of the milieu. Images, colors, and textures all hold particular energies that affect the atmosphere. The charisma of art on the walls is a primary transformative element in the studio because it can convey the message that the group is a safe place.

For many of the clients I have worked with in art-based groups, healing has been a process of transforming destructive, self-defeating energy into creative, life-affirming energy. One of the core purposes of art therapy groups is to activate this nourishing force. The healthy, creative energy seeps into clients' lives in many different ways and it is impossible to predict just how it will manifest itself for each group member. Still, after many years of observation I know the studio or group room works a kind of inexplicable magic. In a sense, the walls of the group room should be a living gallery, always changing and re-forming, providing a powerful and yet unspoken metaphor for the purpose of the place. The studio is a constantly evolving, aesthetic milieu comprised of images and interactions that shape the group's life. When clients enter the group they ought to be greeted by images that invite participation in the healing activity of communal art making. I do not mean to imply that the images on the walls are always comfortable. Sometimes the presence of disturbing imagery can convey the message that the group is a safe place that can embrace many aspects of life, both the pleasant and the disturbing.

Another important element of the creative space is the presence and condition of art materials and equipment. Art materials play a critical role in the design, implementation, and final product of an artwork. It is a serious error to regard the media as only a means to an end, or as a way to get group members involved in talking to one another. The materials and tools used in art-based group work need to be of acceptable quality in order to avoid conveying the meta-message that the creative processes and products are not really valued. In situations where there are budgetary constraints it is better to limit the range of materials and tools rather than to select inexpensive media that communicate such a message.

Different materials, of course, evoke distinctly different psychic states. Materials are the carriers of the emotional states of the artist, and the possibilities are endless. I often encourage clients to combine traditional art materials with found objects—damaged cast-off furniture, shards of broken pottery, shattered mirrors, and other simple objects—to create multimedia artworks that capture the essence of the group member's experience of life. The presence of adequate art materials and an array of miscellaneous objects in the group room help to generate the creative energy of the milieu. Art therapy group work should not be limited to colored markers on white paper and magazine image collages; it must engage materials of many kinds in order to foster the sense of safety and artistic contagion that clients so need.

Co-Leading Art-Based Groups

When I was in training to become a group leader, the model presented to me was that of a solo art therapist facilitator. The leader's tasks were to maintain the structure of the session, integrate new members into the group, introduce artistic experiences, and facilitate verbal discussion of clients' artworks. In this model, the leader was a benevolent, guiding authority figure. For years I imitated this model, and I preferred to work alone and maintain an autocratic stance in my groups. One benefit of this solitary leadership style was that it forced me to carefully focus on the creative process and the unique content of clients' artwork, the psychodynamics of individual group members, and the relationships that emerged in sessions. Another positive result was that because I was alone, I felt a measure anxiety each time I entered the art therapy group room. This served to sensitize me to clients' anxieties, and to remind me how difficult the work was that we were about to undertake. A third benefit was that I provided group members with a single focal point for their projections and feelings related to authority figures, and, finally, the solitary model allowed me to provide a consistent style of direction.

Although there were advantages to working alone, there were also some drawbacks. In moments of intense conflict it was difficult to maintain the objective distance needed to dispassionately observe the group interactions. The amount of information that emerged during sessions—images, responses, clients' affects, and intra-and interpersonal dynamics—was sometimes overwhelming. Whenever I was not able to attend a session due to vacation or illness, my absence caused significant disruptions to the flow of the group. I sometimes experienced intense feelings about clients that were difficult to sort through on my own, even with supervision. Sometimes I was overwhelmed by group members' feelings and I found it difficult to provide a secure, contained environment for clients. I also found that I had emotional blind spots.

Later on in my career I had the opportunity to develop co-therapy relationships and I have learned that there are also pluses inherent in co-leadership. "Leading a group can be a lonely experience at times, and the value of meeting with a co-leader for planning and processing should not be underestimated" (Corey, 2004, p. 49). In all good relationships, there must be a solid core of understanding and acceptance of the other. Ideally, the co-therapy relationship serves as a vessel that holds the norms, images, history, mores, and feelings of the group. The relationship must be resilient and flexible in order to provide the necessary support for the group members.

There are a number of advantages to co-leadership. Multiple leaders can support and model creative engagement in self-expression in diverse ways. Co-leaders may bring a wider range of technical artistic expertise. Group members benefit from the varied approaches and life experiences of multiple therapists. The leaders often have different views on particular situations and this serves to provide perspective and balance. Co-leaders bring their own unique strengths and sensibilities and group members may benefit from these differences.

Furthermore, co-leaders can alternate between active participation and observation. They can model respectful relationship skills through their interactions. If one of the co-leaders is absent, the group can continue without disruption. Participants can receive artistic responses and feedback from multiple perspectives instead of one. Finally, if one of the co-leaders is male and the other is female, they can serve as symbolic parental figures and provide significant reparative experiences for group members.

The primary disadvantages of co-leadership arise when the leaders are not able to create an effective and collegial working relationship. It is terribly important that co-leaders establish a relationship based on mutual respect and trust. If respect and trust are lacking, the group members are likely to sense dissonance, and the group will inevitably act out this absence.

It is crucial that co-leaders meet regularly to discuss their relationship, how they feel about working with one another, how they see the group functioning, and how they use their art to enhance the group experience. Ideally, co-leaders will meet immediately before and after group sessions to plan and reflect on the group's process. When co-leaders fail to meet in this way, it is a sign that there may be problems in their relationship that ought to be addressed for the good of the group.

Debra, the Boys, and I

Debra DeBrular and I worked as co-therapists with groups of older adolescent boys for several years. Prior to her joining the group, I had been leading it alone for several months. In preparation for her entry, we discussed how we felt about the nurturing role she would bring to the group. Debra saw herself as a naturally maternal figure who related in an open, warm way with clients. Within a few weeks of her initial session, the group members were responding to Debra as if she were the mother of the group. Overall, the clients' feelings about her were positive, but there were moments of hostility and negativity. In both such instances, however, significant themes and feelings related to women emerged naturally in each client's artwork and were dealt with effectively in the group. Although the clients' feelings about the maternal figure were potent and often conflicted, the work that Debra and I had done in the preparatory phase of our relationship gave group members freedom to express themselves directly.

After several months had passed, the boys come into a session spewing foul and abusive language that was devaluing of women. Such hostile language was atypical in the group milieu and I grew angry at their vulgarity. At the same time, I was keenly aware of feeling protective of Debra. One of the boys suggested that we work on a mural together and draw a wall with graffiti. We began by covering a large sheet of brown paper (8' x 4') with red and brown chalk. We then smeared the colors together in order to represent a brick wall. The graffiti that covered the wall was hostile and sexually offensive. My anger at the group increased.

Debra's contribution to the wall, however, was an image of a small frail vine growing. When we had finished drawing and began to discuss the work, she talked about the vine. She said that it felt feminine and made her aware that she was the only woman in the group. It suddenly struck me that Debra and I had spent a lot of time talking about her mothering role in the group, but we had not discussed the sexual aspects of her being the only woman.

When we met in our usual post-group discussion, we wondered if the clients were indirectly trying to tell us that they could no longer tolerate this absence in Debra and my relationship. We committed to a process of examining the impact of gender on our relationship, which led to many discussions about the effects of her femininity and my masculinity on the group. Interestingly, there was no further instance of vulgar acting out by the boys after she and I dealt with those issues in our relationship.

In subsequent group sessions the clients were able to artistically explore issues related to their masculinity and the mysteries of relating to girls in more beneficial ways.

Paradoxically, leading art-based therapy groups is a simple and yet difficult and complicated endeavor. Although leaders may strive to keep the group safe and predictable, ultimately it is impossible to predict what will happen in the complex interplay of human interactions and art materials. Whether leading alone or with a co-therapist, I strive to keep things simple in terms of what I initiate in my groups, and then to be as open, sensitive, and adaptable as possible in responding to the limitless forms of expression that arise as group members make and respond to art. The bottom line expectation is that we will express ourselves artistically. I have learned the importance of moderation in leadership, and I know that whatever psychological or emotional issues I am comfortable with in my life, the group will also be able to address. If there are things that I am not comfortable with personally, groups will sense this and not take up those issues. Clearly, I want groups to be free to explore whatever life themes are necessary. This is why it is so important for group leaders to continually work to be self-aware. I strive to always be attentive to individual group members and their artworks, while at the same time encouraging others to respond to their peers' work in creative ways.

Chapter XV

BECOMING A LEADER OF
ART-BASED GROUPS

I am convinced that the only ways to become an effective leader of art-based therapy groups are to (a) observe an experienced leader in action, (b) participate as a member of a training group, (c) utilize personal art therapy, (d) constantly self-reflect, (e) continuously engage in art making, and (f) receive skillful supervision.

Watching Don Jones

I was fortunate to be mentored by Don Jones, ATR, HLM, one of the early pioneers of art therapy in the United States. During my apprenticeship with Don, I was able to watch closely as he facilitated a minimum of two or three art-based group therapy sessions per day with persons suffering a wide range of psychiatric illnesses. There were groups comprised of relatively high functioning adults who were struggling with various neurotic disorders, groups of adolescents made miserable by behavioral and emotional disorders, and groups made up of clients afflicted with severe psychoses and personality disorders. In the end I amassed more than one thousand hours of direct observation. Concurrently, I was a member of a student training group that Don facilitated.

Although at the that time I was anxious to move beyond the confines of observation and try my hand at leading groups, I now understand the enormous benefit of watching an experienced therapist art work. Of particular significance were the post-session discussions. There is no better time for art-based group leaders to teach students than in the hour immediately following a session. I treasure the many things I learned as I asked Don why he had redirected the client to his or her art process, why he had made a certain comment, why he had withheld comments, why he had initiated a creative process in response to a client's work, and on and on.

The form that observation takes during training is dependent upon the facilities and resources of the graduate art therapy program. Some educators prefer that students watch art-based group sessions through a one-way mirror. Other programs make use of videotaped sessions that are subsequently discussed in the context of seminars. I prefer, whenever possible, to have students participate as members of client groups. Regardless of format, it is imperative that clients are not only informed about the presence of observers and their purpose but also give their consent. One other format for observation occurs when students participate as members of their own art-based group and are thus able to experience the process of the group, watch the group leader in action, and subsequently discuss the session from an academic perspective.

Art-Based Groups for Graduate Art Therapy Students

In the graduate art therapy programs where I have taught, I have led students in art-based groups that also function as classes. These group classes have provided students with experiences that are not available in many other learning environments. In essence, there are dual learning objectives. On the one hand the student is studying how art-based groups work, and on the other, how they personally interact with and respond to their peers, to art processes, and to the totality of the interactions that occur. The advantage of this kind of educational experience is that students are able to learn at an experiential and emotional level rather than solely intellectually. They learn firsthand the power of making and sharing art in a group—how this can be used to heal. They experience their own struggles with self-disclosure, the importance of openness, and the contagious flow that communal creative engagement allows. They creatively explore their strengths and weaknesses and have to wrestle with exposing their vulnerabilities and their capacity for compassion. Perhaps most importantly, students learn about the role of the leader by becoming aware of their feelings about the power and knowledge they ascribe to the group leader or course instructor (Yalom, 2005).

For over 30 years I have led art-based groups for students and have invariably found them to be an invaluable teaching process. This form of learning, in which a student is both the studier and the object of study, is often without precedent for most students and nearly all express initial resistance. Still, it has been my experience that the great majority of students look back on group class as one of the highlights of their educational journeys. The success of art-based group classes depends upon the ability of the leader or instructor to maintain clear expectations, structure, and appropriate professional boundaries.

When I have discussed my art-based group classes with colleagues I often have heard them express reservations regarding this kind of learning process. Yalom (2005) discussed such misgivings as follows:

> These warnings are, I believe, based on irrational premises, for example: that enormous amounts of destructive hostility would ensue once a group unlocks suppressive floodgates, or that a group would constitute an enormous invasion of privacy as forced confessionals are wrung one by one from each of the hapless trainees. We know now that responsibly led groups facilitate communication and constructive working relationships. (p. 554)

In my experience, art-based group classes provide students with opportunities to enrich and deepen their relationships with their peers by offering a venue in which to be genuinely open to one another. Ultimately, art therapy involves the formation of intimate relationships through shared art making, and students should demand that their tuition be refunded if they are not afforded such opportunities. The educational guidelines of the American Art Therapy Association assert that programs must teach (a) theoretical and experiential understanding of group art therapy and counseling methods and skills, (b) principles of group dynamics, (c) therapeutic factors, (d) member roles and behaviors, (e) leadership styles and approaches. (f) selection criteria, and (g) short- and long-term group process (AATA, 2007).

I believe that it is impossible to adequately teach these things without an art-based group experience for students. Further, it can be argued that it is unethical for art therapists to ask their clients to do something that they have not done themselves. Because this is an educational requirement, the question of whether or not such classes should be voluntary or mandatory is a moot point. Thus, it is very important that the group class be introduced and explained to students in such a way that they consider it to be relevant to their professional and personal goals. During the first meeting I always tell the students that the purpose of the class is to help them experience the power of art-based group process, to learn about the dynamic elements of leadership, and to explore their own reactions to group art making. The class is not meant to provide therapy, although it may indeed be quite therapeutic. I promise them that we will not cross the boundary between therapy and education, but that I will help them walk right up to that line.

My Flag

Midway through my apprenticeship with Don Jones I began to paint again, at his insistence. I had done little work artistically for a year or two before entering the art therapy educational program. I was ambivalent about the painting that developed over the next few weeks. One day, I would look upon it with pride, and the next day, I found it trite. When the piece was nearly done, I shared my ambivalence about it with Don and he suggested that I bring the painting to the student group when it was finished. Not surprisingly, I both looked forward to and wished to avoid sharing the piece with my peers.

Figure 9. Internship Painting

The painting (see Figure 9 & Plate 9) is a medley of images surrounding a large vertically placed eye. I found many of the details personally interesting. One exception, however, was the section that was a reworking of a still life theme that I had painted dozens of times before. When the student group gathered around my painting, I gave a brief overview of what I thought was significant. Describing the still life section, I said, "This is something I used to paint a lot. It really doesn't mean anything." I was irritated that when I completed my synopsis, Don suggested we begin by focusing our attention on the still life. The images include a bowl of fruit, wine bottle, and soiled American flag nailed to a wall.

Don asked, "Could you free associate on these images?"

I said, " I think this section relates to me being an objector to the Vietnam War. I've done similar paintings a number of times. I am not sure it really means much of anything else." I then suggested that we move on to more intriguing segments of the painting.

Patiently, Don maintained his focus on the still life images. He asked, "Bruce, can you give the American flag a voice and speak from its perspective?"

I hesitated, unsure of what to say.

Don asked, "Flag, how do you feel about having been nailed to this dirty wall?"

I began to sweat. As I spoke for the flag, I burst forth with anger toward the son-of-a-bitch who had so defiled it. The more I said, the angrier I became, until finally I began to shake and couldn't speak at all.

In a gentle voice, Don asked, "Bruce, have you ever seen that flag before?"

I was stunned. I had seen it, not only in many of my paintings, but lying neatly folded in my mother's cedar chest. It was the flag that had covered my father's casket. I wept; 24 years of loss, disappointment, and anger came bubbling to the surface. Suddenly all the protest songs I had sung, marches I had joined, and slogans I had shouted seemed to have nothing to do with conscious moral indignation over the Vietnam War, and everything to do with feelings I had kept hidden away about growing up without a father. My peers in the group sat with me, let me cry, and let me know that it was okay. That painting changed my life.

I learned so much in that one session of the student group. I learned about the power of artistic expression to change lives. I learned about the gentleness of Don's leadership style. I learned the joy of being held by my colleagues in the group. True, I had read about all of these things, and I knew them in my head prior to that experience, but I did not really know them in my heart until that day. Again, it is important to note that Don did not offer me therapy in that context, but the session was indeed therapeutic.

Recurrent Themes from Student Groups

Art-based groups for students typically include many of the themes that arise in client groups, but because they are educationally focused they also have some unique attributes. In my experience, student groups frequently wrestle with three issues: (a) an intense desire to be seen as competent, (b) ambivalence about changing the nature of their relationships with one another from classmates to members of a group, and (c) covert competition with one another. Consequently, they often resist being open to one another out of fear that their vulnerabilities and perceived weaknesses will result in a negative professional judgment from the group leader or their peers. Compounding this fear is the reality that the faculty member or group leader will, in many circumstances, grade them on their participation and mastery of skills.

It is nearly impossible for group members to avoid competency, competition, and relationship issues. Making matters even more difficult is the likelihood that they have other classes together, engage in outside social activities with one another, and sometimes romantic relationships develop. These factors exacerbate tensions within the group. Student groups react to these tensions in a variety of ways, but most common is an unspoken covenant of denial: The group members deny the existence of competition and insist that all members are equal. As the issues inevitably arise and are commented on by the group leader there is often a sense of shared resentment of the leader, as if he or she is just stirring up difficulties. The phenomenon of group denial, coupled with group members' assertions that they are all equal, is in effect a defensive leveling process that can lead to a sense of creative paralysis. It is incumbent upon the group leader to guide the members toward deeper and more authentic relationships with one another.

The Leader's Tasks

The leader of art-based student groups has daunting responsibilities. The leader must serve as a role model, shaping and building the culture of the student group, while at the same time attending to the educational mission of the group. The fundamental approach to these tasks, however, does not stray from the essential principles of art-based group work outlined in the first chapter of this book. For example, the leader is well advised to maintain focus on the process of making art in order to create a sense of ritual, provide psychological safety, and promote interpersonal emotional risk-taking. Students will inevitably try to turn the group into a quasi supervision session, or attempt to reduce it to an intellectual exercise. To counteract these efforts the group leader must continually assert that making art with others is a safe way to express painful, frightening, and other difficult feelings— even feelings of inadequacy and competitiveness. Student groups are an excellent venue for creating a sense of community and are well served when the group leader is committed to making art as a way to symbolize and express feelings regarding interpersonal relationships.

Due to the overarching purpose of art-based student groups to educate, the group leader is in a unique position to experiment with artistic techniques that foster the members' senses of personal and communal empowerment. The leader also has the opportunity to model an attitude of nonjudgmental curiosity and excitement about the group process that can help students confront competitiveness and their misgivings regarding competency. When the group leader is able to create a culture of artistic contagion this allows members to establish genuine positive regard for one another and to experience gratifying and pleasurable aspects of making art in the presence of their peers.

The question of who should lead an art-based training group is one that demands careful consideration. In an ideal world the group leader would serve that function alone; that is, a group leader would not interact with trainees in other contexts. This ideal allows the group members and the group leader to form their relationships in the context of the group experience without the hindrance of extraneous roles. However, it has been my experience that such circumstances are rare in graduate art therapy educational programs. Most often the group leader is a member of the faculty who also teaches other courses and may have supervisory and other administrative duties. This is not an insurmountable problem, but it is a reality that must be addressed.

As noted earlier, the group class experience is an important process in the students' educational career and the leader serves as an influential role model. The leader should be a seasoned practitioner with extensive group experience. The principal criteria for selection of the leader are his or her personal qualities and leadership skills. It is an extremely daunting task to provide potent art-based group experiences while simultaneously adhering to the educational objectives of the group. Students are often hesitant to fully engage in the process because they are intimidated by the presence of the leader, who must evaluate their competency. This dual role problem must be dealt with openly and repeatedly. Training group leaders need to assure the group that despite their dual roles they will do everything they can to keep their focus on the work of the group and maintain confidentiality.

In my career, I have often found myself wearing many hats with group members: graduate program director, academic advisor, supervisor, course instructor, research mentor, and author of textbooks they are using in other courses. These various roles inevitably cause students to view me as a figure with much authority. Every student reacts to this in unique ways. Some attempt to ingratiate, some respond with distrust, some adopt an attitude of continual challenge, and others play out dependency issues. All of these attitudinal responses are grist for the mill of the group process. I have found that my most effective response to students' attitudes is openness and so I look for appropriate opportunities for self-disclosure. In the words of Yalom (2005), self-disclosure provides an avenue "to give the members more on me than I have on them." He continued, in so doing, I model openness and demonstrate both the universality of human problems and how unlikely it would be for me to adopt a judgmental stance toward them" (p. 556). My experience has taught me that when I can be genuinely open students will eventually respond in kind. Just as one image begets another, so too openness begets openness. Thus, I always make art along with group members, and I authentically share my feelings and responses with them.

Personal Art Therapy

Although art-based groups are a must for would-be group leaders, as noted earlier, they ought not serve as a venue for students to receive personal therapy. Still, as graduate students begin to practice group leadership a host of issues arise that may indicate the need for personal art therapy or individual psychotherapy as a component of the educational experience. A number of educators stress that art therapy trainees need to have some experience of what it is like to be a client. They reason that because the art therapist is one of the most powerful components in the art-based group it is imperative that he or she be fully self-aware. Personal art therapy can help students explore their reasons for becoming art therapists and group leaders, and it can help them examine their values, needs, and motivations artistically. Personal psychotherapy can also be of tremendous support to students as they enter the world of group leadership.

Group Leaders Making Art

There has been much written in art therapy literature regarding the question of whether or not art therapists should make art alongside clients. Art therapists must also wrestle with the question of whether or not to make art in the company of their clients. For group leaders, making art or refraining from making art in a group is an interesting professional boundary dilemma. This is a question that has been widely discussed in the art therapy professional community (see, e.g., Haeseler, 1989; McNiff, 1992; B. Moon, 2009; C. Moon, 2002; Rubin, 1998; Wadeson, 1980). Some group leaders assert that there are very few instances when they have chosen to not participate in the process of making art with clients (e.g., McNiff, 1992). In my book, *Existential Art Therapy: The Canvas Mirror*, I posited that the group leader's art making can be critical in establishing the therapeutic culture. "The doing of art is my ritual, a reenactment of my personal journey. My willingness and enthusiasm for the ritual is contagious and it both afflicts and affirms, challenges and assures the client that the journey is worthwhile" (B. Moon, 1995, p. 47). However, Wadeson (1980) and others have warned against making art alongside clients because they believe it can be an intrusion into the therapeutic process. Wadeson stated:

Usually I don't, for several reasons. First, the field of exploration is the client's life, not mine. It's a matter of role. Second, for those clients who feel inadequate in art, my more experienced drawing might prove intimidating. Third, . . . the processing of my picture or sculpture would take up valuable time. (p. 42)

Whether or not leaders choose to make art in their groups has significant impact upon the therapeutic culture. Either of these approaches can be effective if the best interests of the clients have been carefully considered. If leaders choose to create artwork alongside their clients, they must be vigilant to ensure that their artistic participation does not dilute, interfere with, or in some way negatively influence the group process for clients. If group leaders choose not to make art with their clients they have to be attentive to the effects of their nonparticipation. A group leader's passive or watchful stance may interfere with group members' ability to use art expression freely. The choice to not make art may intensify the power differential between leader and client and be detrimental to the group process.

When group leaders are struggling to maintain appropriate boundaries in a group context, they ought to ask themselves this question: How will my art making, or lack thereof, be of help to the group? Art-based group leaders ought to endeavor to always keep the needs of their clients in the foreground as they consider this question. Establishing and maintaining professional roles requires honest self-assessment. Self-understanding in relation to professional boundaries can be stimulated through carefully selected artistic tasks.

Despite the arguments for and against art making alongside clients, I have always made art when leading groups and, as discussed in earlier sections of this book, I have found this to be an important factor in establishing a culture of artistic contagion. From my perspective, leaders of art-based therapy groups have no right to ask group members to do something that they do not do themselves. I believe that it is imperative that group leaders model active and authentic engagement in their own art practices.

My primary art practices include painting, songwriting, digital video, and poetry. I have, at times, used each of these self-expressive modes as vehicles to enhance self-awareness, as aids in establishing empathic relationships with group members, as outlets for my own feelings that are often stirred by a group, and as starting points for imaginative interpretive interactions with group members. As a group leader, my primary focus must always be on the clients. Thus, my art making while in a group is always centered on issues that are relevant to the group's work.

Supervision

Supervised experiences are essential to becoming an art-based group leader. They also are an important way for experienced practitioners to maintain competencies required to adequately carry out their professional responsibilities. "Supervision in the training and continuing education of art therapists is considered to be essential to professionalism" (Malchiodi & Riley, 1996, p. 21). Supervision entails helping neophyte art therapists understand their group leadership style, develop their abilities to self-reflect, and deepen their understanding of art therapy group theory and practical applications. The ultimate goal of art therapy supervision is the integration of these different areas of learning, leading to the development of skillful art-based group leaders.

The word *supervision* is derived from the Latin *super* (over) and *videre* (to watch, to see). *Webster's New World Dictionary* (1988) defined supervision as the action, process, or occupation of supervising; a critical watching coupled with directing activities or a course of action (p. 1345). A supervisor is one who oversees, who watches over the work of another and assumes a measure of responsibility for the quality of the work. Contained within these definitions of supervision and supervisor are three implicit and distinct functions of art therapy supervision: administrative, educational, and role modeling.

The *administrative function* of supervision refers to the supervisor's responsibility to monitor procedural tasks related to the functioning of the art-based groups. Some of the questions that arise in relation to administrative functions are: Does the supervisee start and end the group on time? Is the supervisee adequately prepared for the session? Are the art materials organized in such a way as to facilitate the expressive process? Is the supervisee able to appropriately document the content of group sessions? The *educational function* of supervision refers to the supervisor's duty to structure and promote the development of the supervisee's professional knowledge and growth through reflection upon art-based group therapy experiences. The supervisor works to establish an environment in which the supervisee is able to benefit from the wisdom, experience, and knowledge of the supervisor. The *role-modeling* function of supervision refers to the responsibility of the supervisor to serve as a positive professional example for the supervisee. As role models, supervisors seek to establish a supportive and expressive supervisory milieu in order to nurture the supervisees' professional competencies, identities, and morale. At the same time, supervisors model art therapy professionalism and that in turn fosters self-worth in their supervisees.

Mentor Model of Supervision

The administrative, educational, and role-modeling functions of supervisory relationships are complementary. A *mentor model* of supervision is created when the administrative, educational, and role-modeling functions are properly addressed. The mentor model of supervision involves the establishment of a supportive relationship in which the mentor is regarded as a significant source of affirmation, wisdom, and expertise for the supervisee. The mentor is equally dedicated to passing on and receiving information to and from the supervisee. The mentor is an authority on group leadership who oversees the progress of the supervisee, while simultaneously maintaining an attitude of mutuality with the supervisee. The mentor has technical knowledge, experience, and the capacity to contain and make sense of the swirling emotional currents and intellectual predicaments of the supervisee that inevitably arise in the course of leading a group.

In many ways the mentor serves the supervisee as an observing ego. Carrigan (1993) noted that supervision is "an intensive personal relationship, yet communication between the two parties must remain on a supervisory level," going on to point out that this can sometimes result in "an unequal relationship that allocates most of the responsibilities and power to the supervisor, while the intern may be in danger of being disempowered" (p. 134). In the supervisory relationship, it is the supervisee's responsibility to report on experiences in the art-based group, to have feelings toward clients and the group process, and to have ideas about the course the group should take. It is the mentor's responsibility to "be with" the supervisee (Moustakas, 1995, pp. 84-85), to reflect and sort through the meanings of the supervisee's experiences.

In many ways, the mentor and supervisor's role is one of being a concerned caretaker. Boszormenyi-Nagy and Krasner (1986) discussed the therapist's role as analogous to the supervisor's role with supervisees. "The therapist-client relationship falls short of the symmetry of friendship, for example. Therapy may provide moments of genuine meeting between two people. Still, the degree of investment and the level of expectations between them are always uneven" (p. 395). Supervisors need to convey an unruffled, objective, and yet warmly accepting attitude toward supervisees, who are immersed in the multiplicity of communications they receive from their clients' images, interactions, and words in the course of art-based group work. Group leaders often find themselves experiencing equal measures of awe, inspiration, and emotional turmoil. Sometimes neophyte group leaders feel overwhelmed by their clients' images, verbalizations, and behaviors in the group. At such times, supervisees need the detached support and guidance of the mentor in order to sort through their reactions to clients and group processes.

Art-based group leaders are exposed to the intense anguish, rage, loneliness, needs, and deep longings of their clients. Novice and seasoned group leaders alike can be overwhelmed by their encounters with such powerful forces. In such instances the supervisor's observing ego provides a buffer that aids the supervisee in developing an objective view of the intense artistic expressions that occur in group work. In this way the mentor creates a "holding environment" (Winnicott, 1960, pp. 140–152) for the supervisee and provides the emotional security so essential to the group leader's professional growth and the art-based group's functioning.

In many ways the supervision session becomes a microcosm of the art-based group, and the supervisor can obtain valuable information about the supervisee's behavior in a group by paying attention to his or her behavior in supervision sessions. Yalom (2005) referred to this as a parallel process. My experience has taught me that the best way to connect to this parallel process is by engaging the supervisee in art making about the group in the context of the supervision session. So much happens in an art-based group session that is metaverbal, thus it is important that supervision also employ modes of communication that are not reliant solely on verbalization. There is such an abundance of data that comes from a group session that both supervisee and supervisor must be selective in their focus and the responsive art process is extremely helpful in terms of filtering and identifying the most salient topics.

Summary

Becoming an effective art-based group leader is an arduous task. It entails many hours of direct observation of an experienced group leader, active participation as a group member in a training group class, personal art therapy, serious self-reflection, authentic art making, and supervised clinical work. After 35 years of leading and co-leading groups I still find myself learning new things about this work and I am always fascinated by the images and interactions that emerge as people make art together. The experience is never dull. Learning to be a group leader is a challenging and ongoing career-long process.

Chapter XVI

MATERIALS AND MEDIA IN
ART-BASED GROUPS

Historically, when materials and media have been discussed in art therapy literature in reference to group work the focus has typically been limited to drawing materials, paints, clay, and collage (see, e.g., McNiff, 2003; Riley, 2001; Rubin, 1998; Skaife & Huet, 1998; Waller, 1993). Relatively little attention has been given to the use of photography, found objects, fibers, digital video, sound, and other technology-based media. Similarly, discussion of art-making processes have for the most part been focused on drawing, paintings, sculpture, and collage. There have been few if any references to installation art, assemblage, puppetry, altered book making, performance, collaborations, or conceptual art.

C. Moon (2010) addressed the absence of a broad and inclusive survey of media and material applications that reflects the diverse range of practices evident in contemporary art. She included contributions from a few practitioners who work in art-based group formats. Feen-Calligan, McIntyre, and Sands-Goldstein (2009) discussed dollmaking as a therapeutic process, and Chilton (2007) explored using altered books in art therapy groups with adolescents. Still, the bulk of art therapy group literature has included limited discussion of media other than those noted above.

The paucity of literature regarding media and materials in art therapy can at least partly be attributed to the relatively short history of the profession and concern with being regarded as a legitimate a psychotherapy practice. C. Moon (2010) also called for a critical examination of the ways that media and material use has played out in art therapy. She asserted that in the majority of the literature, the discussion of material use is limited to an unselfconscious focus on so called "high art"–specifically painting, drawing, and clay sculpture–in spite of the fact that persons receiving the services of art therapists often are from marginalized groups for whom these materials provide little that is culturally relevant or economically feasible. C. Moon's critique has forced us to examine the media routinely utilized in art-based group work. We have to question the efficacy of introducing costly materials such as acrylic paint and canvas to clients who cannot afford the basic necessities of life. As we consider the range of materials and media used it is most important to keep in mind the primary motivations for art making in art-based groups: creative self-expression, interpersonal metaverbal communication, catharsis, mastery, cognitive structuring, emotional organization, creation of community, gratification, promotion of positive regard for self and others, self-transcendence, and expression of the ultimate concerns of existence. Clearly, these motivations can find form in a multitude of materials and media and I am becoming increasingly interested in how diverse arts practices can be integrated into group work.

Contemporary arts practices have taught us that virtually any material has the potential to be an agent of change in both individual applications and group work. Art-based group leaders need not be confined to the traditional materials–chalk, paint, clay, and collage. I encourage us to question our use, or lack of use, of nontraditional materials and to ask ourselves questions regarding the materials we make available in art-based group work. We need to think deeply and critically about the range of media currently utilized in the art world, considering all perspectives, particularly those previously underrepresented in our literature.

In a small number of the vignettes included in this text I have referred to using nontraditional media and art practices such as found objects, performance, and vocalization. I confess, however, that the majority of my illustrations have been restricted to drawing and painting. It has only been in the last few years that I have expanded my repertoire of media and I regard that as a shortcoming of this text. Many contemporary artists provide models for meaningful engagement with a wide range of materials that promote subjective expression and engagement with the world. At the time of this writing I have begun to question the economic ramifications of our media, and I am striving to behave more as an artist-role model rather than a mere consumer of traditional art materials. Although this is a relatively new area of interest, I find that clients in my art-based groups are enriched when I expose them to the expressive possibilities of found objects, installation artwork, performance, digital media, eco art, conceptual art, and the host of possibilities found in collaborative art practices.

Again, contemporary arts practices have taught me that practically any material has the potential to be a positive mediator of change for clients in art-based group work. Although I will no doubt continue to use the old standbys—oil pastels, tagboard, and paint—in art-based groups, I will constantly be on the lookout for new media and new art processes to incorporate into my group practice.

EPILOGUE

This book has been a long time in the making. The taproots of art-based group therapy are art and group psychotherapy. The bulk of art therapy group literature has focused on the group psychotherapy root, and less attention has been given to our artistic lineage. In this book I have revisited some of the artistic roots of group work and attempted to demonstrate an approach to art-based group therapy through clinical vignettes. It is my sincere wish that the artistic root should receive the attention it deserves.

Some of my art therapy colleagues assert that the art therapy profession must emulate the techniques and language of other professions in order to be taken seriously in the health care marketplace. Although I am not opposed to art therapists doing whatever they must to attain professional security, I do worry that our identity as art therapists has been compromised. I am concerned by those who would steer future generations of art therapy group leaders away from the art of art-based group work, toward the verbal techniques and interventions that are the domain of other disciplines.

In hindsight, I see now that this book, along with everything else I have written, is a call to art therapists to embrace the artistic dimensions of our professional identity and use creativity when we present ideas about the discipline of art therapy. As I complete this book, which strives to articulate nearly four decades of art-based group therapy practice, my overwhelming sense is that the work is continually reforming. This feeling of ongoing creation is tied to the foundation of art's healing power that resides in its ability to constantly transform life anew. I have experienced revitalization in writing this book and I hope that readers will experience a similar effect.

People throughout the world are discovering the efficacy of art-based group therapy and this bodes well for the future of art therapists and clients alike. Transformation through communal creative expression is one of humankind's oldest phenomena, and I hope this book honors the ancient healing tradition of making art in the company of others. Still, I urge readers to be critical of anything in this book that feels heavy handed or dogmatic. I encourage all to be as open as possible to the process of discovery, and your own contributions to art therapy group work. Consider the ideas presented in this text as suggestions intended to incite your own explorations.

The turbulent environment of health care in the United States, from the mid-1970s through the first decade of the twenty-first century, has provided an exceptional laboratory for the ideas about art-based group work presented in this book. It has been my pleasure to share stories from the trenches of my work with groups of adult and adolescent clients, from inpatient hospitals, residential treatment facilities, colleges and universities, and private practice, in this edition. I hope my work here serves to fill an empty place in the collection of our professional literature.

Bruce L. Moon
Mundelein, IL

Plate 1. J.T.'s Brown

Plate 2. Basket Detail #1

Plate 3. Basket Detail #2

Plate 4. The Names

Plate 5. The Names

Plate 6. Coal and Diamond

Plate 7. Untitled Painting from Opening Colloquium

Plate 8. Darien's First Painting

Plate 9. Internship Painting

REFERENCES

Allen, P. (1995). *Art is a way of knowing.* Boston, MA: Shambala.

American Art Therapy Association. (2007). *Masters Education Standards.* Alexandria, VA: American Art Therapy Association, Inc.

Boszormenyi-Nagy, I., & Krasner, B. (1986). *Between give and take: A clinical guide to contextual therapy.* New York, NY: Brunner/Mazel.

Buber, M. (1970). *I and thou.* New York, NY: Simon & Schuster.

Campbell, J. (1968). *The masks of God: Creative mythology.* New York, NY: Penguin Books.

Carrigan, J. (1993). Ethical considerations in a supervisory relationship. *Art Therapy: Journal of the American Art Therapy Association, 10,* 130–135.

Chilton, G. (2007). Altered books in art therapy with adolescents. *Art Therapy: Journal of the American Art Therapy Association, 24*(2), 59–63.

Corey, G. (2004). *Theory and practice of group counseling* (6th ed.). Belmont, CA: Thompson Brooks/Cole.

Corey, M., Corey, G., & Corey, C. (2008). *Groups: Process and practice* (8th ed.).Pacific Grove, CA: Brooks/Cole Cengage Learning.

Couch, R. D., & Childrers, J. H. (1987). Leadership strategies for instilling and maintaining hope in group counseling. *Journal for Specialists in Group Work, 12*(4), 138–143.

Curtis, G. (2007). *The cave painters: Probing the mysteries of the world's first artists.* New York, NY: Anchor.

Donne, J. (1999). *Devotions upon emergent occasions: and, Death's duel.* New York, NY: Vintage. (Original work published 1623)

Frankl, V. E. (1955). *The Doctor and the soul.* New York, NY: Alfred A. Knopf.

Fromm, E. (1956). *The art of loving.* New York, NY: Harper & Row.

Gussow, A. (1971). *A sense of place.* San Francisco, CA: Friends of the Earth.

Haeseler, M. (1989). Should art therapists create artwork alongside their clients? *The American Journal of Art Therapy, 27,* 70–79.

Hamburg, D. A. (1963). Emotions in perspective of human evolution. In P. Knapp (Ed.), *Expressions of emotions in man.* Symposium held at the meeting of the American Association for the Advancement of Science in New York on December 29–30, 1960. New York, NY: International Universities Press.

Hanes, K. (1982). *Art therapy and group work: An annotated bibliography.* Santa Barbara, CA: Greenwood Press.

Henley, D. (1997). Expressive arts therapy as alternative education: Devising a therapeutic curriculum. *Art Therapy: Journal of the American Art Therapy Association, 14,* 15–22.

Herrera, H. (2002). *Frida: A biography of Frida Kahlo.* New York, NY: Harper Perrenial.

Hillman, J. (1975). *Re-Visioning psychology.* New York, NY: Harper Collins.

Hillman J. (1989). *A blue fire: Selected writings.* New York, NY: Harper & Row.

Janson, H. W. (1971). *History of art.* New York, NY: Harry N. Abrams.

King, S. (1988). *Misery.* New York: Signet

Lantz, J. (1993). *Personal communication.* Worthington, Ohio

Lasch, C. (1979). *The culture of narcissism.* New York, NY: W.W. Norton.

Liebmann, M. (2004). *Art therapy for groups: A handbook of themes and exercises* (2nd ed.). New York, NY: Brunner-Routledge.

Malchiodi, C., & Riley, S. (1996). *Supervision and related issues: A handbook for professionals.* Chicago, IL: Magnolia Street.

Marin, P. (1975). *The new narcissism.* New York, NY: Harpers.

McNeilly, G. (2006). *Group analytic art therapy.* Philadelphia, PA: Jessica Kingsley.

McNiff, S. (1992). *Art as medicine.* Boston, MA: Shambhala.

McNiff, S. (2001). *Earth angels: Engaging the sacred in everyday things.* Boston, MA: Shambhala.

McNiff, S. (2003). *Creating with others.* Boston, MA: Shambhala.

McNiff, S. (2004). *Art heals: How creativity cures the soul.* Boston, MA: Shambhala.

McNiff, S. (2009). *Integrating the Arts in Therapy: History, Theory, & Practice* Springfield, IL: Charles C Thomas

Meier-Graefe, J. (1987). *Vincent van Gogh: A biography.* Mineola, NY: Dover Publications.

Moon, B. (1990). *Existential art therapy: The canvas mirror.* Springfield, IL: Charles C Thomas

Moon, B. (1995). *Existential art therapy: The canvas mirror.* (2nd ed.). Springfield, IL: Charles C Thomas

Moon, B. (1998). *The dynamics of art as therapy with adolescents.* Springfield, IL: Charles C Thomas.

Moon, B. (2009). *Existential art therapy: The canvas mirror.* Springfield, IL: Charles C Thomas.

Moon, C. (2002). *Studio art therapy: Cultivating the artist identity in art therapy.* Philadelphia, PA: Jessica Kingsley.

Moon, C. (2010). *Materials and media in art therapy: Critical understandings of diverse artistic vocabularies.* New York, NY: Routledge.

Moore, T. (1992). *The care of the soul: A guide for cultivating depth and sacredness in everyday life.* New York, NY: HarperCollins.

Moustakas, C. (1995). *Being-In, Being-For, Being-With.* New York, NY: Jason Aronson.

Pelta, K. (2001). *Rediscovering Easter Island.* Minneapolis, MN: Lerner Publishing Group.

Prinzhorn, H. (1922). *Artistry of the mentally ill.* New York, NY: Springer-Verlag.

Riley, S. (2001). *Group process made visible: Group art therapy.* Philadelphia, PA: Brunner-Routledge.

Rogers, C. (1951). *Client-centered therapy: Its current practice, implications and theory.* London, England: Constable.

Rubin, J. (1998). *Art therapy: An introduction.* New York, NY: Brunner/Mazel.

Rutan, S., Stone, W., & Shay, J. (2007). *Psychodynamic group therapy* (4th ed.). New York, NY: Guilford Press.

Skaife, S., & Huet, V. (Eds.). (1998). *Art therapy groups: Between pictures and words.* New York, NY: Routledge.

Steinbach, D. (1997). *A practical guide to art therapy groups.* New York, NY: Routledge.

Steiner, R. (1999). *The art students league of New York: A history.* Saugerties, NY: CSS Publications.

Wadeson, H. (1980). *Art psychotherapy.* New York, NY: John Wiley & Sons.

Waller, D. (1993). *Group interactive art therapy: Its use in training and treatment.* New York, NY: Routledge.

Webster's new world dictionary (3rd ed.). (1988). New York, NY: Simon & Schuster.

Winnicott, D. W. (1960). *The maturational processes and the facilitating environment: Studies in the theory of emotional development.* New York, NY: International Universities Press.

Yalom, I. (2005). *The theory and practice of group therapy* (5th ed.). New York, NY: Basic Books.

SUGGESTED READINGS

Alter-Muri, S., & Klein, L. (2007). Dissolving the boundaries: Postmodern art and art therapy. *Art Therapy: Journal of the American Art Therapy Association, 24*(2), 82–86.

Backos, A. K., & Pagon, B. E. (1999). Finding a voice: Art therapy with female adolescent sexual abuse survivors. *Art Therapy: Journal of the American Art Therapy Association, 16*(3), 126–132.

Buchalter, S. I. (2004). *A practical art therapy.* New York, NY: Jessica Kingsley.

Camilleri, V. A. (2007). *Healing the inner city child: Creative arts therapies with at-risk youth.* Philadelphia, PA: Jessica Kingsley.

Chinn, P. L., & Watson, J. (1994). *Art and aesthetics in nursing.* New York, NY: National League for Nursing Press.

Collie, K., Backos, A., Malchiodi, C., & Spiegel, D. (2006). Art therapy for combat-related PTSD: Recommendations for research and practice. *Art Therapy: Journal of the American Art Therapy Association, 23*(4), 157–64.

Collie, K., & âubraniç, D. (1999). An art therapy solution to a telehealth problem. *Art Therapy: Journal of the American Art Therapy Association, 16*(4), 186–193.

Couch, R. D., & Childers, J. H. (1987). Leadership strategies for instilling and maintaining hope in group counseling. *Journal for Specialists in Group Work, 12*(4), 138–143.

Dennison, S. T. (1988). *Activities for adolescents in therapy: A handbook of facilitating guidelines and planning ideas for group therapy with troubled adolescents.* Springfield, IL: Charles C Thomas.

Drapeau, M., & Kronish, N. (2007). Creative art therapy groups: A treatment modality for psychiatric outpatients. *Art Therapy: Journal of the American Art Therapy Association, 24*(2), 76–81.

Feen-Calligan, H., McIntyre, B., & Sands-Goldstein, M. (2009). Doll in art therapy: Applications in grief recovery, professional identity, and community service. *Art Therapy: Journal of the American Art Therapy Association, 26*(4), 177–182.

Graham, M., & Sontag, M. (2001). Art as an evaluative tool: A pilot study. *Art Therapy: Journal of the American Art Therapy Association, 18*(1), 37–43.

Hartz, L., & Thick, L. (2005). Art therapy strategies to raise self-esteem in female juvenile offenders: A comparison of art psychotherapy and art as therapy approaches. *Art Therapy: Journal of the American Art Therapy Association, 22*(2), 70–80.

Henley, D. R. (2000). Blessings in disguise: Idiomatic expression as a stimulus in group art therapy with children. *Art Therapy: Journal of the American Art Therapy Association, 17*(4), 270–275.

Howie, P., Burch, B., Conrad, S., & Shambaugh, S. (2002). Releasing trapped images: Children grapple with the reality of the September 11 attacks. *Art Therapy: Journal of the American Art Therapy Association, 19*(3), 100–105.

Lark, C. V. (2005). Using art as language in large group dialogues: The TREC model. *Art Therapy: Journal of the American Art Therapy Association, 22*(1), 24–31.

Luzzatto, P., & Gabriel, B. (2000). The creative journey: A model for short-term group art therapy with posttreatment cancer patients. *Art Therapy: Journal of the American Art Therapy Association, 17*(4), 265–269.

Lyshak-Stelzer, F., Singer, P., St. John, P., & Chemtob, C. M. (2007). Art therapy for adolescents with posttraumatic stress disorder symptoms: A pilot study. *Art Therapy: Journal of the American Art Therapy Association, 24*(4), 163–169.

Makin, S. (2000). *Therapeutic art directives and resources.* London, England: Darien Kingsley.

Malchiodi, C. A. (2003). *Handbook of art therapy.* New York, NY: Guilford Press.

Malchiodi, C. A. (2008). *Creative interventions with traumatized children.* New York, NY: Guilford Press.

McKaig, A. M. (2003). Relational contexts and aesthetics: Achieving positive connections with mandated clients. *Art Therapy: Journal of the American Art Therapy Association, 20*(4), 201–207.

Murphy, J. (2001). *Art therapy with young survivors of sexual abuse: Lost for words.* Philadelphia, PA: Taylor & Francis.

Pifalo, T. (2002). Pulling out the thorns: Art therapy with sexually abused children and adolescents. *Art Therapy: Journal of the American Art Therapy Association, 19*(1), 12–22.

Pifalo, T. (2006). Art therapy with sexually abused children and adolescents: Extended research study. *Art Therapy: Journal of the American Art Therapy Association, 23*(4), 181–185.

Ponteri, A. K. (2001). The effect of group art therapy on depressed mothers and their children. *Art Therapy: Journal of the American Art Therapy Association, 18*(3), 148–157.

Riley, S. (1994). *Integrative approaches to family art therapy.* Chicago, IL: Magnolia Street.

Rubin, J. A. (2005). *Artful therapy.* Hoboken, NJ: John Wiley & Sons.

Rubin, J. A. (2005). *Child art therapy: 25th anniversary edition.* Hoboken, NJ: John Wiley & Sons.

Sandle, D. (1998). *Development and diversity: New applications in art therapy.* New York, NY: Free Association Books.

Sweig, T. (2000). Women healing women: Time-limited, psychoeducational group therapy for childhood sexual abuse survivors. *Art Therapy: Journal of the American Art Therapy Association, 17*(4), 255–264.

Testa, N., & McCarthy, J. B. (2004). The use of murals in preadolescent inpatient groups: An art therapy approach to cumulative trauma. *Art Therapy: Journal of the American Art Therapy Association, 21*(1), 38–41.

Turetsky, C. J., & Hays, R. E. (2003). Development of an art psychotherapy model for the prevention and treatment of unresolved grief during midlife. *Art Therapy: Journal of the American Art Therapy Association, 20*(3), 148–156.

Vick, R. M. (1999). Utilizing prestructured art elements in brief group art therapy with adolescents. *Art Therapy: Journal of the American Art Therapy Association, 16*(2), 68-77.

Wadeson, H., & Wirtz, G. (2005). The hockey/art alliance. *Art Therapy: Journal of the American Art Therapy Association, 22*(3), 155–160.

INDEX

155

Here and now, 57–60, 114
Herrera, H., 4
Hillman, J., xvi, 12
History of art-based group therapy, xii–xiv
Honoring experience, 20, 21, 61, 101
Hope, 8, 23–27, 96
Huet, V., x, xii, 135
Hull House, xiii

I

I-It, 68, 72
Imagination, 31, 57, 60, 73, 74, 79, 90
I-Thou, 68, 112

J

Janson, H. W., 58
Jones, D. 48, 108, 121, 124
Judgment, 7, 66, 84, 127, 128

K

Kapitan, A., xvii
King, S., 101
Krasner, B., 133

L

Lantz, J., 35
Lasch, C., 6
Leadership, 11, 69, 107–120, 123–124, 126, 129
Liebmann, M., x
Lesley University, xvii
Looking in the mirror, 99–106
Loneliness, 4, 54, 62, 64, 106, 133

M

Maladaptive patterns, 16
Malchiodi, C., 131
Marywood University, x, xvii
Materials and media, 135–137
McIntyre, 135
McNeilly, G., x
McNiff, S., 3, 4, 5, 6, 14, 20, 27, 67, 73, 74, 75, 79, 100, 101, 129, 135
Meaning, 4, 68, 81, 87
Meirle-Graefe, J., xii

Mentor model of supervision, 132–134
Metaverbal, xvi, 13, 23, 30, 31, 111, 133, 136
Miller, A., xvii
Mindfulness, 87, 88, 106
Model, 67, 68, 80, 84, 100, 101, 114, 118, 127, 128, 130, 136
Moon, B., 3, 6, 11, 12, 23, 37, 68, 99, 129
Moon, C., 11, 129, 135, 136
Moore, T., 12
Moreno, J., xiii
Mount Mary College, x, xvii, 74
Moustakas, C., 111, 132–133
Movement response, 77

N

Narcotics Anonymous, xiv

O

Occam's razor, 107
Opening colloquium, 74–80
Openness, 112, 115, 122, 128
Ormont, L., xiii

P

Pain, 8, 27, 31, 48, 61, 66, 73, 87, 96, 100, 101, 106–111, 127
Passion, 110
Pelta, K., 4
Personal art therapy, 129
Personal characteristics of leaders, 110, 111
Pleasure, 14, 57, 73, 79, 88
Polarities, 61, 102
Pratt, J., xiii
Predictability, 13–15, 21, 115
Prinshorn, H., 88, 91

R

Reciprocal response, 80
Recurrent themes, 126
Regard for others, 9, 67–72
Resist, 46, 68, 69, 74, 75, 89, 96, 107, 109, 110, 123, 126
Response, 4, 5, 69, 79, 80
Responsive art making, 13, 77, 80, 88, 115, 118, 122
Rhythm, 13, 74, 75, 79, 94